GREAT BRITAIN IN 22 DAYS

A STEP-BY-STEP GUIDE AND TRAVEL ITINERARY

BY RICK STEVES

Published by
John Muir Publications
Santa Fe, New Mexico

Copyright © 1986 by Rick Steves
Maps Copyright © 1986 by John Muir Publications
All rights reserved. Printed in U.S.A.
ISBN 0-912528-52-4

Maps Jim Wood
Cover Jennifer Dewey
Design/Production Mary Shapiro
Typography Casa Sin Nombre

Thanks to my eternal travel partner,
research assistant—and wife—Anne.

CONTENTS

Tour Route

0 10 20   40   60
MILES

HIGHLANDS
INVERNESS
LOCH NESS
(16)
BEN NEVIS
SCOTLAND
OBAN
(15)
LOCH LOMOND
GLASGOW
EDINBURGH (17,18)

HADRIAN'S WALL
(19)
DURHAM
BELFAST
LAKES DISTRICT
(13,14)
ISLE OF MAN
NORTH YORK MOORS
(20)
YORK (21)
BLACKPOOL
(12)
DUBLIN
ENGLAND
IRELAND
SNOWDONIA
(11)
IRONBRIDGE GORGE
(10)
COVENTRY
(9)
WARWICK
STRATFORD
(8)
CAMBRIDGE
(22)
COTSWOLD VILLAGES
WALES
BLENHEIM PALACE
(7)
CARDIFF
(5)
BATH
LONDON
(1,2,3)
STONEHENGE
WELLS
(6)
(4)
GLASTONBURY
SALISBURY

HOW TO USE THIS BOOK

This book is the tour guide in your pocket. It lets you be the boss by giving you the best 22 days in Britain and a suggested way to use that time most efficiently.

Great Britain in 22 Days is for do-it-yourselfers who would like the organization and smoothness of a tour without the straight-jacket. It's almost having your cake and eating it too.

The "22 Days" books originated (and are still used) as handbooks for those who join me on my "Back Door Europe" tours. Since most large organized tours work to keep their masses ignorant while visiting many of the same places we'll cover, this book is handy for anyone taking a typical big bus tour—but wanting also to maintain some independence and flexibility.

This plan is maximum thrills per mile, minute and dollar. It's designed for travel by rental car, but is adaptable to train (see p. 90). The pace is fast but not hectic and is designed for the American with limited time who wants to see everything but doesn't want the "if it's Tuesday this must be Edinburgh" craziness. The plan includes the predictable "required" biggies (Big Ben, Stratford, Wordsworth's cottage and Stonehenge) with a good dose of "Back Door" intimacy—cozy Cotswold villages, windswept Roman lookouts, Gaelic folk pubs, angelic boys' choirs —mixed in.

Great Britain in 22 Days is balanced and streamlined, avoiding typical tourist burn-out by including only the most exciting castles and churches. I've been very selective. For example, we won't visit both Oxford and Cambridge—just the best of the two. The "best," of course, is only my opinion. But after ten busy years of travel writing, lecturing and tour guiding, I've developed a sixth sense of what tickles the traveler's fancy. I love this itinerary. I get excited just thinking about it.

Of course, connect-the-dots travel isn't perfect, just as color-by-number painting ain't good art. But this book is your smiling Scotsman, your Bobbie in a bind, your handbook. It's your well-thought-out and tested itinerary. I've done it—and refined it—many times on my own and with groups (most recently in October and November 1985). Use it, take advantage of it, but don't let it rule you.

Read this book before you begin your trip. Use it as a rack to hang more ideas on. As you plan and study and travel and talk to people, you'll fill this book with notes. It's your tool. The book is completely modular and is adaptable to any trip. You'll find 22 units—or days— each built with the same sections:

1. **Introductory overview** for the day.
2. An hour-by-hour **Suggested Schedule** recommended for that day.
3. List of the most important **Sightseeing Highlights** (rated: ▲▲▲Don't miss; ▲▲Try hard to see; ▲Worthwhile if you can make it).
4. **Transportation** tips and instructions.
5. **Food** and **Accommodations**: How and where to find the best budget places, including addresses, phone numbers, and my favorites.
6. **Orientation** and an easy-to-read **map** locating all recommended places.

7. **Helpful Hints** on shopping, transportation, day-to-day chores.
8. **Itinerary Options** for those with more or less than the suggested
time, or with particular interests. This itinerary is *rubbery!*

At the end of the book are special chapters on such things as English
history and politics, post-tour options, tips on telephoning, car rental,
driving, etc.

Travel Smart
This itinerary assumes you are a well-organized traveler who lays departure groundwork upon arrival in a town, reads a day ahead in this book,
uses a larger directory-type guidebook and the local tourist info offices,
and enjoys the hospitality of the British people. Ask questions. Most
locals are eager to point you in their idea of the right direction. Use the
telephone, wear a moneybelt, use a small pocket notebook to organize
your thoughts and make simplicity a virtue. If you insist on being con-
fused, your trip will be a mess. If you expect yourself to travel smart,
you will.

Cost
This trip's cost breaks down like this: A basic round-trip USA–London
flight ($400—800, depending on the season and where you fly from). A
three-week car rental (split between two people, including tax, insurance, and gas) or three weeks of rail and bus travel—$300. For room
and board figure $30 a day, double occupancy—$660. This is more
than feasible, and if necessary, you can travel cheaper (see *Europe
Through the Back Door* for the skills and tricks of traveling cheap). Add
$200 or $300 fun money and you've got yourself a great British adventure for under $1,800.

When to Go
July and August are peak season—best weather and the fullest schedule
of tourist fun, but very crowded, most difficult, and more expensive.
Most of us travel during this period (Maybe that's why it's so crowded...?), and this book tackles peak season problems, especially that
of finding a room.
   "Shoulder season" travel (May, early June, September, and early October) is ideal. If at all possible, plan a shoulder season trip for minimal
crowds, decent weather, sights and tourist fun spots still open, and the
joy of being able to just grab a room almost whenever and wherever
you like.
   Winter travelers find absolutely no crowds, but many sights and accommodations are closed or run on a severely limited schedule. The
weather can be cold and dreary, and nightfall will draw the shades on
your sightseeing well before dinner time.
   In my experience, British weather is reliably unpredictable (but
mostly bad) and July and August are not much better than shoulder
months. Conditions can change several times in a day but rarely is the
weather extreme. Daily averages throughout the year fall between 42
and 70 degrees, and temperatures below 32 or over 80 are cause for
headlines.

Prices & Times

I've priced things in pounds (£) throughout the book. There are 100 pence (p) in each pound (£), and a pound at this writing is worth about $1.50. I haven't cluttered this book with many minor prices (e.g. specific admission fees and student discounts etc.). Small charges of less than a dollar shouldn't affect your sightseeing decisions.

Prices as well as hours, telephone numbers, and so on, are accurate as of November 1985. Things are always changing and I've tossed timidity out the window, knowing you'll understand that this book, like any guidebook, starts to yellow before it's even printed. Britain is more stable than most European countries but do what you can to double-check hours and times when you arrive.

The hours listed are for peak season. Many places close an hour earlier in off season. Some are open only on weekends or are closed entirely in the winter. Confirm your sightseeing plans locally—especially when traveling between October and May. Many sights shift into winter schedules, closing earlier, when daylight savings time is over in late October.

Ugly Americanism

We travel all the way to Great Britain to experience something different—to become temporary locals. Americans have a knack for finding certain truths to be God-given and self-evident—things like cold beer, a bottomless coffee cup, long hot showers, driving on the righthand side of the road, bigger being better. One of the beauties of travel is the opportunity to see that there are logical, civil, and even better alternatives.

If there is a British image of you and me, we are big, loud, a bit naive, aggressive, and rich. (The American worker earns twice what his British counterpart does, and taxes, unemployment and the cost of living are all higher for the British worker).

Still, I found warmth and friendliness throughout Great Britain. An eagerness to go local and an ability—when something's not to my liking—to change my liking, made sure I enjoyed a full dose of this British hospitality.

Scheduling

Your overall itinerary is a fun challenge. Read through this book and note special days (festivals, colorful market days, closed days for sights etc.). Sundays have pros and cons as they do for travelers in the USA (special events, limited hours, shops and banks closed, limited public transportation, no rush hours). Saturdays are virtually weekdays. Popular places are even more popular on weekends—especially sunny ones, which is sufficient cause for an impromptu holiday in the soggy British Isles).

It's good to alternate intense and relaxed periods. Every trip (and every traveler) needs at least a few slack days. I followed the Biblical "one in seven" idea . . . religiously. . . on my last trip.

To give you a little rootedness, I've minimized one night stands. Two nights in a row, even with a hectic travel day before and after, is less grueling than changing accommodations daily.

The daily suggested schedules and optional plans take many factors into account. I don't explain most of those but I hope you take the schedules seriously.

Car Rental
If you plan to drive, rent a car through your travel agent well before departure. Car rental for this tour is cheaper in the USA than in England. You'll want a weekly rate with unlimited mileage. Plan to pick up the car at Heathrow Airport on Day 4 and drop it off 19 days later at Cambridge. Remember, if you drop it early or keep it longer, you'll be credited or charged at a fair, pro-rated price. Also keep in mind that you may drop the car at any location if you have a change of plans. Budget, Hertz, Avis, Kenning and Godfrey Davis all allow Heathrow pick-ups and Cambridge drops. See which is cheapest through your agent.

I normally rent the smallest, least-expensive model (e.g., Ford Fiesta). For a bigger, more roomy and powerful inexpensive car, move up to the Ford 1.3-liter Escort category. For peace of mind, I splurge for the CDW insurance (collision damage waiver) which gives a zero-deductible rather than the standard $1,000-deductible. Remember, mini-buses are a great budget way to go for 5 to 9 people.

Recommended Guidebooks
This small book is only your itinerary handbook. To really enjoy and appreciate these busy three weeks, you'll also need a directory-type guidebook and some good maps. I know it hurts to spend $30 or $40 on extra books and maps, but when you consider the improvements they'll make in your $2,000 vacation—not to mention the money they'll save you—not buying them would be perfectly "penny-wise and pound (£) foolish." Here's my recommended list of supplemental information needed:
General low-budget directory-type guidebook—that is, a fatter book than this one, listing a broader range of accommodations, restaurants, sights, etc. Which one you choose depends on your budget and style of travel. My favorite by far is *Let's Go: Great Britain and Ireland*, written and thoroughly updated every year by Harvard students (new editions come out around March). *Let's Go* covers big cities, villages, countryside, art, entertainment, budget room and board, transportation, etc. It's written for students on a student's budget and even though I'm neither, I use it every year. If its youthful approach isn't yours, then try Arthur Frommer's *Britain on $25 a Day*.
Cultural and sightseeing guide—The American Express "Pocket Guide to England and Wales" and the AmExCo guide to London by Mitchell Beazley are compact and packed with handy info including a rundown on local art, history and culture, a list of all major sights, maps, and a helpful listing of hotels and restaurants for those with a little more money. The Michelin tall green guide to London is also good.
Europe Through the Back Door (by Rick Steves) gives you the basic skills, the foundations which make this demanding 22-day plan possible. Chapters on: minimizing jet lag, packing light, driving vs. train travel, finding budget beds without reservations, changing money, theft and the tourist, travel photography, long distance telephoning in Eu-

rope, ugly-Americanism, traveler's toilet trauma, laundry, and itinerary strategies and techniques. The book also includes special articles on 32 exciting nooks or undiscovered crannies which I call "Back Doors." Six of these are in the British Isles.

Books and Maps to Buy in England—Most English bookstores, especially in touristed areas, have a good selection of maps. I found a "Road Atlas" book very useful for my basic overall needs (3 miles to one inch, covering all of Britain, put out by the Ordinance Survey or by Bartholomew, about $7). For this itinerary, I'd also pick up much more detailed maps for the Cotswold region, North Wales, Windemere Lakes District, West Scotland, and North York Moors.

Foyles' Bookstore near Piccadilly Circus in London has the best selection of guides and maps anywhere in Britain. WH Smith stores, the "English B. Dalton's," found in nearly every city, carry a good selection of guidebooks, maps, and local information.

As you travel you'll find racks of tempting little books at virtually every stop. The traditional finale of all British tourist attractions is a cute gift and book shoppe. Local tourist offices also abound providing lots of good printed material. Take advantage of this wealth of fascinating and helpful information. For a complete list of all you'll need that can be picked up in one stop at the London Tourist Office, see page 18.

Freedom

This book's goal is to free you, not chain you. Please defend your spontaneity like you would your mother. Use this book to sort Britain's myriad sights into the most interesting, representative, diverse, and efficient 22 days of travel. Use it to avoid time- and money-wasting mistakes, to get more intimate with Britain by traveling without a tour—as a temporary local person. And use it as a point of departure from which to shape *your* best possible travel experience.

Anyone who has read this far has what it takes intellectually to do this tour on their own. Be confident, militantly positive, relish the challenge and rewards of doing your own planning.

Send Me a Postcard, Drop Me a Line. . . .

While I do what I can to keep this book accurate and up-to-date, things are always changing. If you enjoy a successful trip with the help of this book and would like to share your discoveries (and make my job a lot easier), please send in any tips, recommendations, criticisms or corrections. All correspondents will receive a year's subscription to our *Back Door Travel* quarterly newsletter (it's free anyway. . .), and recommendations used will get you a free copy of my next edition.

Thanks, and Bon Voyage!

BACK DOOR TRAVEL PHILOSOPHY
AS TAUGHT IN EUROPE
THROUGH THE BACK DOOR

Travel is intensified living—maximum thrills per minute and one of the last great sources of legal adventure. In many ways, the less you spend the more you get.

Experiencing the real thing requires candid informality— going "Through the Back Door."

Affording travel is a matter of priorities. Many people who "can't afford a trip" could sell their car and travel for two years.

You can travel anywhere in the world for $20 a day plus transportation costs. Money has little to do with enjoying your trip. In fact, spending more money builds a thicker wall between you and what you came to see.

A tight budget forces you to travel "close to the ground," meeting and communicating with the people, not relying on service with a purchased smile. Never sacrifice sleep, nutrition, safety or cleanliness in the name of budget. Simply enjoy the local-style alternatives to expensive hotels and restaurants.

Extroverts have more fun. If your trip is low on magic moments, kick yourself and start making things happen. Dignity and good travel don't mix.

If you don't enjoy a place it's often because you don't know enough about it. Seek out the truth. Recognize tourist traps.

A culture is legitimized by its existence. Give a people the benefit of your open mind. Think of things as different but not better or worse.

Of course, travel, like the world, is a series of hills and valleys. Be fanatically positive and militantly optimistic.

Travel is addicting. It can make you a happier American, as well as a citizen of the world. Our Earth is home to five billion equally important people. That's wonderfully humbling.

Globetrotting destroys ethno-centricity and encourages the understanding and appreciation of various cultures. Travel changes people. Many travelers toss aside their "hometown blinders," assimilating the best points of different cultures into their own character.

The world is a cultural garden. We're working on the ultimate salad. Won't you join us?

ITINERARY

DAY 1 Arrive in London, visit the tourist information office to lay the groundwork for the next three weeks, get set-up in your "bed and breakfast" and take an evening walk through the heart of London.

DAY 2 Take the two-hour introductory double-decker bus tour of London before the 11:30 changing of the guard at Buckingham Palace. Then walk through the Piccadilly area to colorful Covent Gardens for lunch. Spend the afternoon touring the Tower of London with a Beefeater guide and take a close look at the crown jewels. Then take the Thames cruise from the bloody tower to Westminster, landing at the foot of Big Ben. Check out Westminster Abbey, possibly visit the Halls of Parliament to see the House of Commons in action, grab some pub grub for dinner and finish the day enjoying one of London's plays.

DAY 3 London has so much to see. Spend the morning touring the British Museum. Walk down Fleet Street for a pub lunch with London's harried newspaper crowd. Climb to the summit of St. Paul's, pop in to view the action at "Old Bailey," the high criminal court complete with powdered wigs and robes, or tour the London Stock Exchange before finishing your sightseeing day in the Museum of London.

DAY 4 Pick up your rental car at Heathrow airport to avoid crazy London driving, and drop by Salisbury to see its cathedral. Wander through the mysterious Stonehenge and Avebury stone circles before joy-riding through several picturesque villages and into Bath.

DAY 5 Tour Bath's Roman and Medieval mineral baths before a coffee break in the elegant Pump Room. Follow a local guide for two hours of history and highlights of England's trend-setting old world Hollywood. Spend the afternoon browsing and touring England's greatest collection of costumes—three hundred years of fashion history.

DAY 6 Today, sidetrip south exploring the haunted and entertaining Wookey Hole Caves, Wells with its medieval center and striking cathedral, and mystical Glastonbury—mythical home of Avalon, King Arthur and the Holy Grail. Evening free in Bath.

DAY 7 We'll drive into Wales, through its capital of Cardiff and to St. Fagan's Folk Museum—a park full of Welsh culture, restored old houses, and an intimate look at this fascinating culture. After a scenic drive up the Wye River Valley, past Tintern Abbey and through the Forest of Dean, we'll set up at Stow-on-the-Wold in the heart of the Cotswold Hills.

DAY 8 Spend half the day savoring the most delicious of England's villages, the quintessence of quaint. Then visit Blenheim Palace.

DAY 9 After a morning in Shakespeare's hometown, Stratford, we'll tour England's finest medieval castle at Warwick and see the inspirational Coventry Cathedral—a charred ruin from the "blitz" with a shiny new church built more with love than with nails.

DAY 10 Today is devoted to the birthplace of the Industrial Revolution. The Ironbridge Gorge on the Severn River is a series of museums that take the visitor back into those heady days when Britain was racing into the modern age and pulling the rest of the West with her. Then it's into the romantic beauty of North Wales, setting up in Ruthin.

DAY 11 Circling scenic and historic North Wales, we'll tour a woolen mill, the Caenarfon Castle, awesome Mount Snowdon and a bleak slate mine, arriving home in time to indulge in a medieval Welsh banquet— complete with harp, singing, mead and daggers for meat-eating.

DAY 12 From the Garden of Eden to the garden of Hedon-ism, we'll drive to Blackpool—England's Coney Island—for a look at the most popular tourist attraction in Britain . . . that all Americans skip. Six miles of fortune tellers, fish 'n chips, amusement piers, beaches, warped mirrors and hordes of English. It's recess!

DAY 13 For another splash of contrast, we'll drive into the pristine Lake District, inspiration for Wordsworth, with enough natural beauty to make anyone a poet. After a short cruise, and a six-mile walk around the loveliest of these lovely lakes, we'll check into a remote farmhouse B&B.

DAY 14 A pilgrimage to Wordsworth's famous Dove Cottage is in order before enjoying a free day to relax, recharge, and take the hike you like.

DAY 15 Now north into Scotland, past bustling Glasgow, along the scenic Loch Lomond for a six hour drive to the Highlands. Blaring bag-pipes and swirling kilts accompany dinner tonight.

DAY 16 Today's all-day joy-ride features the stark beauty of Glencoe, scene of a bloody clan massacre, a drive from coast to coast along the Caladonian Canal and Loch Ness. Even if you don't see the monster, you will tour a grand castle and enjoy some fine Highland scenery. After a visit to Culloden, the site of the last battle on British soil—and the end of Bonnie Prince Charlie and Scottish hopes, you'll zip down from In-verness to Edinburgh.

DAY 17 Edinburgh! one of Europe's most entertaining cities. After a tourist office orientation, we'll cover the Royal Mile, touring the Edin-burgh Castle, the Holyrood Palace—where the queen stays when she's in town—and everything in between. This is the colorful city of Robert Louis Stevenson, Walter Scott and Robert Burns.

DAY 18 There's much more to see and do in Edinburgh: a concert in the park, the elegantly Georgian new town, the best shopping in Scot-land, and an evening of folk music and dance.

DAY 19 Two hours south of Edinburgh, Hadrian's Wall reminds us that Britain was an important Roman colony two thousand years ago. After a walk along Hadrian's ramparts and through a fine Roman museum, it's on to the fascinating Beamish Open Air Museum for a look at life in the dawn of our century. Finally, we'll tour the Durham Cathedral, England's finest Norman church.

DAY 20 After a morning in the lonesome North York Moors with its time-passed villages, bored sheep and powerful landscapes, we'll set up in the city of York in time to enjoy an introductory walking tour by an old Yorker.

DAY 21 York has more than its share of block-buster sights. We'll divide this day between the great York Minster, the Jorvik exhibit—the best Viking museum anywhere—and several engrossing hours in the York Castle Museum—a walk with Charles Dickens and the most eye-opening look at our past you'll ever open your eyes for.

DAY 22 After a three-hour drive to Cambridge, we'll check our bags at the station, turn our car in, and spend the afternoon exploring England's loveliest cluster of campuses. Cambridge, with its sleepy river, lush green grounds, mellow study halls, helpful tourist office and old streets clogged with bicycles, is worth all the time you can muster today before catching the hour long train ride into London. The circle is complete and you've experienced the best 22 days Britain has to offer. Of course, next year you may want 22 more.

City Tours
London
Bath
Edinburgh
York
Cambridge

Churches
Salisbury (spire, Gothic)
Wells (arch, carving, Gothic)
Coventry (WW II reconciliation and modern art)
Durham (best Norman, or Romanesque)
York Minster (windows, undercroft, Gothic)
Cambridge, King's College (windows, fan vaulting, high Gothic)

Castles
Tower of London
Warwick
Caernarfon
Edinburgh

Ancient Sites
Stonehenge
Avebury
Bath, Roman Spa
Hadrian's Wall & Fort

Palaces
Blenheim
Holyrood

Abbeys
Glastonbury
Tintern

Historical Museums
London, Museum of London
London, British Museum
Cambridge, Fitzwilliam Museum
York, Jorvik Viking Exhibit
Bath, Costume Museum
Bath, Georgian House
Wordworth's Dove Cottage
Edinburgh, Several small houses of history along the Royal Mile

Folk Museums
St. Fagan's, Cardiff—Welsh Folk
Ironbridge Gorge—Industrial Revolution
Beamish—Life in 1900
York Castle Museum—Life 1700—1900

Great Wilderness
Cotswold Hills and Villages
North Wales, Snowdon National Park
Lakes District, Cumbria
Scottish Highlands
North York Moors

Miscellaneous Fun and Culture
London Theater
Wookey Hole Caves
Medieval Welsh Banquet
Slate Mine Tour
Evensong service
Blackpool Amusements

DAY 1
FLY TO LONDON

On this busy first day you'll fly halfway round the world, set up and settle in for a night in one of the world's most exciting cities—London.

Suggested Schedule

Depart USA

Arrive at airport in London, travel downtown. Follow "Arrival in London" instructions carefully.

Check into hotel, hostel or Bed & Breakfast.

Visit Tourist Info at Victoria Station (possibly en route to hotel) for London and Britain information and play tickets. Make trip-organizing phone calls from hotel.

Bus downtown to Westminster Bridge for your "first night walk."

(Note: If your plane arrives in the morning, you may have time to take the Round London orientation this afternoon, freeing up some time tomorrow.)

Flying Away
Call the airport before leaving home to be sure your plane's on schedule. Combat boredom and frustration from the inevitable delays and lines by bringing something to do—a book, journal, some handwork. Expect delays and remember no matter how long it takes, flying to England is a very easy, space-age way to get there. If you haven't already read this book carefully from cover to cover, make notes during the flight.
   To minimize jet lag (body clock adjustment, stress):
■ Leave well rested. Schedule a false departure day one day early. Plan accordingly, and, even at the cost of hecticity the day before, enjoy a peaceful last day.
■ During the flight, minimize stress by eating lightly, avoiding alcohol, caffeine and sugar. Drink juice.
■ Sleep through the in-flight movie—or at least close your eyes and fake it (unless you're reading *Great Britain in 22 Days*).

Arrival in London
When you fly to Europe you lose a day. If you left on Friday, you'll land on Saturday. From the airplane, follow the "arrivals" signs to baggage and customs. Heathrow Airport has a reputation for being confusing. Ask questions. (The locals speak English). Collect your baggage and proceed to customs. The customs official will take a quick look at your

passport, ask you a few questions to be sure you're adequately financed and not a spy, and wave you through. After customs you'll pop into throngs of waiting loved-ones. You'll see a Barclays Bank (open 24-hours daily) and an Information desk. Change plenty of money, and buy a £5 bag of 10p coins for phone calls and future parking. At the terminal info desk, pick up a London map, ask about transportation downtown by Airbus or subway and get directions to the Heathrow tourist information office. You might also drop by your car rental agency's desk to confirm your pick-up plans on Day 4. Then follow the signs to the subway, or "underground," (a long walk on a moving ramp), to the T.I. This airport tourist office (open 9:00-6:00 daily) is less crowded than the Victoria Station office downtown. Get whatever info you'd like and consider buying your "Explorer ticket" (to cover your trip downtown), and your "Open to View" ticket. The T.I. is at the subway stop, or you can walk back into the airport to catch the Airbus.

Transportation Downtown

The fastest and easiest cheap way into London is by tube (subway) or Airbus—depending on where your hotel is. Buses leave Heathrow constantly: A1 to Victoria Station, A2 to Paddington Station and A3 to Euston Station with stops along the way (£3). Most of my hotel recommendations are on the A2 Airbus line near Nottinghill Gate.

To save money, buy an Explorer transit ticket at the subway ticket window and use it on this bus ride. This gives you unlimited bus and subway transportation throughout London, including Airbus and subway to and from Heathrow. While the subway works fine, I prefer taking the Airbus into London—there are no connections underground, lovely view from top of the double-decker. The driver will remind you when to get off if you ask him to.

Most flights arrive at Heathrow but some charters go into Gatwick

Airport. Trains shuttle between Gatwick and Victoria Station four times an hour (a 30-minute ride).

Orientation
London, over 600 square miles of urban jungle with seven million struggling people, is a world in itself, a barrage on all the senses, and a place that can make you feel very small. It's much more than museums and famous landmarks. It's a living, breathing organism that somehow manages to thrive.

London Town has changed dramatically in recent years and many visitors are surprised to find how "un-English" it is. Whites are actually a minority now in a city that once symbolized white imperialism. Arabs have pretty much bought out the area north of Hyde Park. Fish and chips shops are now out-numbered by Chinese take-outs (or "fee n' chee shops" as locals call them). Most hotels are run or at least staffed by people with foreign accents, while outlying suburbs are huge communities of blacks, Pakistanis, Indians and Orientals. London is learning—sometimes fitfully—to live as a microcosm of its formerly vast empire.

With just three nights and two days here we'll get no more than a quick splash in this teeming human tidepool. But hopefully, with some quick orientation, we'll get a good sampling of its top sights, history, cultural entertainment and ever-changing human face.

London has all the pitfalls of any big city, but if you're on the ball, informed and well-organized it won't cost a fortune, you won't get ripped-off, and you'll leave ready for the more peaceful countryside but looking forward to your return.

Transportation in London
London's taxis, buses and subway system make a private car unnecessary. In a city this size, you must get comfortable with its public transportation. Don't be timid; dive in, figure it out, take the bull by the horns, and in no time you'll have London by the tail.

Taxis—Big, black, carefully regulated cabs are everywhere. I never met a crabby cabbie in London. They love to talk and know every nook and cranny in town. Rides start at 70p and stay surprisingly reasonable. There are often extra charges (legitimate ones) added on, but usually two or three people in a cab travel at subway prices. If the top light is on just wave one down. Telephoning is unnecessary—taxis are everywhere.

Buses—London's extensive bus system is easy to follow if you have a map listing the routes (as on most tourist maps). Signs at the stops list exactly where the buses go, and conductors are terse but helpful. Ask to be reminded when it's your stop. Just hop on and take a seat (I always go upstairs). You'll be ticketed whenever the conductor gets around to it. Buses and taxis are miserable during rush hours—8-10 am and 4-7 pm. Rides vary from 30p to over a pound.

Subway—The London "tube" is one of this planet's great people movers. Every city map includes a tube map. You'll need it. Navigate by color-coded lines and north (always up on the map) south, east or west. You buy your ticket before descending—at the window or from coin-op machines to avoid the line—then hang onto it, giving it to a checker as you leave the system. Read system notices and signs carefully, ask questions of locals, and watch your wallet. You'll find that "tubing" is by far the fastest long-distance transport in town. It used to be fiercely expensive but now is a reasonable 30p to £1.50 per ride.

Special Money-Saving Transit Tickets
Nearly every tourist should take advantage of one of these subway/bus "go as you please" specials. Available on the spot in subway stations, they give you unlimited transportation on all buses and subways.
Explorer Pass—1 day—£3, 3 days—£8.50, 4 days—£11 and 7 days—£14, covering the entire system including subway and Airbus to and from Heathrow airport.
Travelcard—7 days unlimited coverage within the subway "circle" line for £4. Few tourists take advantage of this, though nearly every major tourist sight is covered in this central circle. The airport trip, unfortunately, isn't covered. Pick this card up in any subway station (photo required). Travelcards are available covering even bigger areas and longer durations.
Cheap day returns—The English love to encourage round trips on train, subway or bus with R/T fares often just barely more than one-way.
    Ask at any tube station for a brochure about special passes. It makes negative sense to prepurchase any of these in the USA. But wise travelers pick them up upon arrival to cover the ride in from Heathrow.

London Information
You can't do London without information. Good guidebooks abound. (I like *Let's Go Britain* and London guides by Michelin, Beazley, and Frommer.) The free London transport and tourist map (available at the Tourist Information office, some subway stations and hotels) is good enough, but the first class map (50p) is ideal.
    Tourist offices are located at Heathrow airport, in Victoria Station (tel. 730-3488, open daily 9:00-8:30, 8:00-10:00 in July and August), at Selfridges on Oxford Street and at Harrods (regular store hours). The Victoria Station office has a great selection of books covering all of Britain, a room-finding service (not cheap), and a helpful staff around with a huge arsenal of fliers, lists, maps and printed advice. They can also sell you theater tickets.
    For the best listing of what's going on this week (plays, movies, exhibitions, concerts, walking tours, protests, what to do with children, restaurants, etc.) pick up a current copy of "What's On"—50p at any newsstand. ("Time Out" and "City Limits" are hip and more opinionated versions of "What's On". You can also telephone 246-8041 for a taped listing of today's happenings.)
    At the tourist info desk, have a check list. Go over your London plans, buy a ticket to a play, and pick up these publications:
    Events and Entertainment, theater guide
    Directory of Tourist Info Centers
    "What's On" (or "Time Out" or "City Limits")
    Quick Guide to London—50p.
Then go around the corner to the National Tourist bookshop.

National Tourist Information
The energetic British Tourist Authority will be opening a large new office just off Piccadilly Circus on Lower Regent Street in 1986. Even so, the Victoria Station tourist office will still have the best travel-in-Britain bookstore for your trip, as well as toll-free information phones for Scotland and Wales. Be sure to drop by here after you visit the London Tourist Information to consider buying info for your whole trip. If you bite the bullet and buy 'em all now, it will save time and confusion since you can study ahead and arrive prepared with proper maps. I'd recommend the following:

■ A Britain Road Atlas (the AA edition) £3.75
■ Let's Go: Britain (if you don't already have it). £7
■ Youth Hostel Association 1986 Guide (if you plan to) £1.25
■ American Express Guides to London and England (each by Beazley) £4.95
■ Stonehenge and Avebury (picture book) £1.25
■ Wales Tourist Map—95p
■ Tourist Guide to North Wales £1.20
■ Tourist Guide to South Wales £1.20
■ Cotswolds Wyedean Official Tourist Map (covering Tintern to Coventry) £1.95
■ Shropshire (Heart of England Tourist board) 95p
■ Lake District Tourist Map (Ordnance Survey) £2.40
■ The Good Guide to the Lakes (Hunter Davies) £2.95
■ Leisure Map Touring Scotland £1.50
(And consider the many enticing guides and maps to London)
That's £35 or $50, but for two people, it's a dollar a day to be really prepared to travel smart. You are your own guide—be a good one.

Accommodations
Cheap, central and comfortable—pick two. With London's great subways, I'll sacrifice centrality for a cheery place that won't ruin my budget. London has hundreds of hotels but few great deals. There's no need, however, to spend a fortune or stay in a dangerous, depressing dump.

Reserve your London room in advance with a phone call direct from the states. Assure them that you'll arrive before 4:00 pm, or send a signed travelers check covering at least the first night. (Include a note explaining that you'll be happy to pay cash upon arrival so they can avoid bank charges if they'll just hold your check until you get there.) Here are a few of my favorites:

Hotel Ravna Gora—Located just across from the Holland Park tube station. Formerly Mr. Holland's mansion, now it's a large B&B run by supporters of the long-exiled King of Yugoslavia. A bit eccentric and well worn—still, you won't find a more comfortable or handy place for the price. Mandy and Rijko take good care of their guests while downstairs the Serbian royalists quaff beer and dream of a glorious restoration some day. Royal TV room, good English breakfast, on the Central tube line, Airbus A2 uphill from Kensington Hilton. Single—£15, Double—£22, Triple—£27, Quads—£36. At 29 Holland Park Avenue, London WII, tel. 727-7725.

Vicarage Private Hotel, 10 Vicarage Gate, Kensington, London W8, tel. 229-4030, is very popular, family-run in a quiet, classy neighborhood midway between Nottinghill Gate and High Street Kensington tube stations near Kensington Palace. Smaller, cozier and more expensive than Ravna Gora. Prices with English breakfast and shower down the hall are: Single—£14, Double—£25, Triple—£32, Quad—£36. Make reservations long in advance with phone call followed by one night's deposit (travelers checks in pounds).

Abbey House Hotel, 11 Vicarage Gate, Kensington, London, W8, tel. 727-2594 is similar in almost every way to its neighbor the Vicarage Private Hotel. A few pounds more expensive. Friendly management. One night deposit required ($50 signed travelers check is fine).

Alba Guest House, 53 Pembridge Villas, London, W11, tel. 727-8910 is very small, friendly and family run in a funky but pleasant locale at the foot of colorful Portobello Road, a block from the Nottinghill subway stop. Run by Raymond Khoo, £24 doubles.

Methodist International House—at 4 Inverness Terrace near Bayswater tube, tel. 229-5101. This Christian residence filled mostly with Third World students is depressing until you see beyond the cracked plaster and worn carpets. If you want a truly world-wide dorm experience give them a call. £10 including breakfast and a great dinner. Don't miss the 10 pm social hour with tea and cookies. Closed for a good part of the year.

Norwegian YWCA (Norsk K.F.U.K.)—For women only (and men with Norwegian passports), this is an incredible value—lovely atmosphere, on quiet stately street, piano lounge, TV room, study, all rooms with private shower, all three meals included, single—£11.50, double—£10, triple—£9, and £8 each in quads. They have mostly quads so if you're willing to share with strangers you're most likely to get a place. Tel. 727-9897, 52 Holland Park, W11 3R5. (I wonder what's easier—a sex change or getting a Norwegian passport?)

Catholic International Chaplaincy—Another gem, open to both men and women but only from mid-June to September 30, Father Maguire provides a TV lounge, study room, self-serve kitchen, garden, English breakfast and a very pleasant atmosphere for £8 in a single or only £6 in a double or triple. He will make reservations (£10 or $20 signed traveler's check deposit) for those staying for a week. Otherwise, call from the airport when you land. Tel. 727-3047, 41 Holland Park, W11 3RP.

Coleman Lodge Hotel—Big, hip, scruffy but comfortable, this was the best cheap hotel I found in the center. Student-oriented, bar, laundry, TV lounge, £8.50 per person in double room with English breakfast. 31 Craven Hill Gardens, W2, Tel. 723-5988, near Lancaster Gate and Bayswater tube stations.

Youth Hostels—London has five or six official and more unofficial hostels. Personally, I'd stick to the official ones, but all are the large, impersonal, regimented big-city variety. They are very popular, always fill up, are equipped with good facilities, and are the cheapest beds in town—under £4.

Harlingford Hotel at 61 Cartwright Gardens, tel. 387-1551, is very well run and comfortable. Located near the British Museum (Russell Square tube) on a crescent with several other good budget B&Bs, £28 doubles.

Holland Park Hotel—The most "hotellesque" of any of these places. Still, Kathy and Steve Keating run this good value with a personal touch. £19 single, £26 double, £36 triple, £42 quad (more with private showers), TVs in each room, English breakfast, quiet, pleasant street, will accept telephone reservations without deposits if you'll arrive by mid-afternoon. 6 Ladbrook Terrace, W11 3PG, tel. 727-8166.

Near Victoria Station—Belgrove Road, Warwick Way and St. George Way are lined with reasonable B&B's.

London

1 - HOLLAND PARK HOTEL
2 - KENSINGTON HILTON, CLOSEST AIRBUS STOP TO RAVNA GORA
3 - CATHOLIC CHAPLAINCY
4 - LADBROOK ARMS PUB (PUB GRUB WITH ATMOSPHERE)
5 - POLICE STATION & POST OFFICE
6 - GEALE'S FISH & CHIPS (FARMER ST.)
7 - LATE-NIGHT SUPERMARKET
8 - GALLEON RESTAURANT - VERY CHEAP. WHERE EDITH BUNKERS GO

WHEN THEIR ARCHIES DIE (AND ARCHIES WHO NEVER FIND THEIR EDITHS)
9 - JUST SOUTH OF MAP IS HIGH ST. KENSINGTON TUBE, COMMONWEALTH INSTITUTE, SLEAZY EARL'S COURT
10 - NORWEGIAN YWCA
11 - KENNING CAR RENTAL
12 - VERY CHEAP PHOTO COPY (USE YOUR HOTEL'S TRAVEL LIBRARY)

NOTE - BUSES 12 & 88 GO FROM HOLLAND PARK AVE & BAYSWATER ROAD TO OXFORD CIRCUS, PICADILLY, TRAFALGAR & WESTMINSTER.

Food

London has plenty of fine restaurants—charging very high prices. If you want to dine (as opposed to eat), check out the extensive listings in "What's On." The American Express London guidebook is a reliable source with more opinions. The thought of a £10 meal generally ruins my appetite so my dining here is mostly limited to unremarkable but wonderfully inexpensive alternatives.

Pub grub is your most atmospheric option. Many of London's 7,000 pubs (I counted them myself one night) serve fresh and tasty buffets under ancient timbers with hearty lunches and dinner costing £3-4. Ethnic restaurants from all over the world more than make up for the basically lackluster English cuisine. Eating Indian or Chinese is "going local" in London. It's also going cheap.

Fish 'n chips are still popular and easy to find. The best fish 'n chips in town in a comfy setting near my recommended B&B's is the very popular **Geale's** at #2 Farmer Street, just off Nottinghill Gate. Open Tuesday-Saturday, 12-3 and 6-11. Get there early for the best selections.

And of course the picnic is the fastest, healthiest and cheapest way to go. There are plenty of good grocery stores and fine park benches in Britain's most expensive city.

First Night Walk

Now that you're set up for the night in London, it's time to enjoy a very relaxed introduction to the city. This walk is a pleasant orientation, and also a great way to stay awake on the jet-lag evening of your arrival.

Catch a bus down to Westminster Bridge (#12 or 88 from Nottinghill Gate, sit on the top deck). Walk halfway across the bridge to view the floodlit Halls of Parliament and Big Ben to get that "Wow, I'm really in London!" feeling. Grab a light dinner at Grandma Lee's Restaurant across from Big Ben next to the tube station.

Then cross Whitehall, noticing the Churchill Statue in the park. (He's electrified to avoid the pigeon problem that stains so many other great statues.) Walk up towards Trafalgar Square. Stop at the barracked and guarded little Downing Street to see #10, home of the British Prime Minister. Break the bobbie's boredom—ask him a question. Just before Trafalgar, drop into the Clarence Pub for a pint of whatever you fancy. From Trafalgar, walk to thriving Leicester Square and continue to Piccadilly.

For seediness, walk through Soho (north of Shaftesbury Avenue) up to Oxford Street. From Piccadilly or Oxford Circus you can taxi, bus or subway home. Why not teach yourself the subway system now? With all this activity, you're more likely to get some good sleep on the traditionally fitful first night of jet lag.

DAY 2
AROUND LONDON

The sights of London alone could easily fill a book like this. Today and tomorrow will be spent enjoying as many of these sights as time and energy will allow. Obviously, this is only a suggested itinerary. You'll have two days in which to pick and choose among all the things listed here.

Suggested Schedule

(pron: "shedule" in England)

8:00 am	Breakfast, subway or bus to Marble Arc.
9:00 am	Catch Round London Tour.
11:00 am	Taxi to Buckingham Palace for 11:00 Changing of the Guard. Or practice a little urban immersion—strolling, window-shopping and people watching your way from Marble Arch along Oxford Street, Regent Street, Soho, Piccadilly and Leicester Square to Covent Gardens.
1:00 pm	Lunch in Covent Gardens—no shortage of intriguing food and colorful surroundings.
2:00 pm	Walk the Strand the the Temple Tube station and subway to Tower Hill. Tour the Tower of London starting with the Beefeater Tour. Don't miss the crown jewels.
5:00 pm	Sail from the Tower to Westminster Bridge enjoying a thirty-minute commentary on the Thames. The Westminster Abbey is open until 6:00 and the Visitors Gallery in the Halls of Parliament is open, when in session, from 6:00. (If you have a play to see or are traveling in summer, this schedule is probably too much unless you're real speedy.)
7:00 pm	Pub dinner near your theater.
8:00 pm	Most plays start at 8:00 pm, enjoy the one of your choice.

Sightseeing Highlights

After considering nearly all of London's tourist sights, I have painfully pruned them down to just the most important (or fun) for a first visit. You won't be able to see even all of these—so don't try to. You'll keep coming back to London. After 15 visits myself, I still enjoy a healthy list of excuses to return.

▲▲**Round London Tour**—This orientation tour is your best intro. The city bus company gives these two-hour "stay on the bus and enjoy a light once over of all the most famous sights with a great commentary" double-decker tours for £3.75. Tours leave daily on the hour from 9:00 to 4:00 plus 6:00 from Marble Arch, Piccadilly Circus and Victoria Station (Grosvenor Gardens). No reservations necessary—or possible.

Walking Tours—Every day several walking tours explore specific slices

of London's past. These are listed in "What's On," and the Tourist Info
has plenty of fliers. You just show up at the announced location, pay
£2, and enjoy two hours of Dickens, the Plague, Shakespeare, Jack the
Ripper, or whatever is on the menu. Evenings feature organized pub
crawls and "ghost walks".

▲▲▲**Tower of London**—Don't miss the entertaining Beefeater tour
(free, leaving regularly from inside the gate). Best armory in Britain is in
the White Tower. Get your armor education in here. Lovely Norman
chapel. Crown jewels are best on earth—and consequently have 2-hour
lines mid-day in July and August. To avoid the crowds, arrive at 9:30
and go straight to the jewels, doing the Tower later. (Tower hours: Open
Mon-Sat 9:30-5:45, Sun 2:00-5:45. The long line moves fast usually, but
is slowest on Sundays.)

Great tourist office across from the Tower entrance. St. Katherine
Yacht Harbor, chic and newly renovated, just past the freshly painted
Tower Bridge with historic boats and mod shops. Classic old pub, the
Dickens Inn, fun for a drink or lunch. Boat tours with a very good com-
mentary sail regularly between Westminster Bridge (behind T.I.) and the
Tower (30 minutes, £1). Best bit of London's Roman Wall just north of
tower. (Tube: Tower Hill).

▲▲▲**Westminster**—The Abbey, Halls of Parliament and Whitehall.

Westminster Abbey is a crowded collection of England's most famous
tombs. Historic, thought-provoking, but a bit over-rated, open 8:00-
6:00, till 8:00 on Wednesdays.

The Halls of Parliament are too tempting to terrorists to be open to
tourists. But you can view the House of Commons when it's sitting,
Monday-Thursday 2:30-10:00 pm.—long waits until 6:00, use St.
Stephens entrance—no bags allowed, call 219-4272 for details. Don't
miss the view from the bridge. You won't actually see Big Ben, the 13-
ton bell (with the famous dong dong dong dong. . .dong dong dong
dong. . .tune) inside the neo-Gothic tower; you'll hear him, though.
And remember, these old-looking buildings are Neo-Gothic—just 100
years old, reflecting the Victorian move away from Neo-classicism and
into a more "Christian," medieval style.

Whitehall, the center of government boulevard, runs from Big Ben to
Trafalgar past lots of important-but-boring buildings. Stop by #10
Downing Street (the British "White House"), the Royal Horse Guard's
(10:00-4:00, 11:00 inspection, 4:00 colorful dismounting ceremony, the
rest of the day—very still, lots of photos), the Banqueting Hall (England's first Renaissance building by Inigo Jones in 1625), and the atmospheric Clarence Pub. The newly opened Cabinet War Rooms, Churchill's underground headquarters during the "Blitz", are fascinating.
Only a 3-minute walk from Big Ben.

▲▲**Trafalgar Square**—London's central square, and a thrilling place to
just hang out. There's Lord Nelson's towering column surrounded by
giant lions made from the melted-down cannons of his victims at
Trafalgar, hordes of people and even more pigeons. The square is the
climax of most marches and demonstrations and the bullseye of the
target-shaped London postal code ("SW7" means to the southwest of
here seven rings or zones). Nearby is The National Gallery with
paintings by Leonardo, Caravaggio, Velazquez, the Impressionists, and

Jan Van Eyck's great Arnolfini Marriage (free, Monday-Saturday 10:00-
6:00, Sunday 2:00-6:00) and the less exciting National Portrait Gallery.
▲▲**Piccadilly**—The "Town Square" of London is surrounded by fascinating streets and neighborhoods. Shaftesbury Avenue and Leicester
Square teem with fun-seekers, theaters, Chinese restaurants and street
singers. Soho, to the north, seethes with sleazier activities and is worth
at least a gawk. Walk up Berwick Street to Oxford Street and check out
the formerly trendy, now tacky Carnaby Street. The shiny new
Trocadero Center has the Guiness World Records Exhibit and the
touristy but fun London Experience movie (10:20 am—10:20 pm daily,
£2). The whole area between Regent Street, Oxford Street, Kingsway
and the Strand is titillating to say the least. Covent Gardens is especially
fun with its buskers, antique shops, liberal bookstores, far-out crowds
and imaginative eateries.
▲**Buckingham Palace** and **Changing of the Guard**—Overrated but
almost required. You'll only see the back side of the palace, as the front
faces a huge and very private park. The royal residence of London is
never open to the public (although if you look sincere and ask the guard
if you can sign the visitor's book, he may escort you in). The changing
of the guard, almost daily in summer at 11:30, is a mob scene. The best
view is from the top of the Victoria Monument. The pageantry and
parading are colorful and even stirring, but the actual changing of the
guard is a non-event. My favorite way to get there is to hop in a big
black taxi and say "to Buckingham Palace, please" as if you're on your
way to tea. Stroll through St. James Park nearby.
▲**Hyde Park**—London's "Central Park" with over 600 acres of lush
greenery, a huge man-made lake, a royal palace (Kensington, worth
touring) and the ornate Neo-Gothic Albert Memorial across from the
Royal Albert Hall. On Sunday mornings, when nearly all other sights are
closed, check out Speaker's Corner, at Marble Arch. This is soap-box
oratory at its best, the grassroots of democracy.
Street Markets—If you like garage sales and people-watching, try to
hit a London Street Market. The tourist office has a complete list. A few
of the best are: Berwick St. (tube: Oxford, Monday-Saturday, produce),
Jubilee Market (tube: Covent Gardens, 9:00-4:00, antiques and bric-a-
brac on Mondays, general miscellaneous on Tuesday-Friday, crafts on
Saturday and Sunday), Kensington Market (tube: High Street Kensington, Monday-Saturday 10:00-6:00, modern and far-out clothing),
Petticoat Lane (Middlesex St., tube: Liverpool St. Sunday, 9:00-1:30,
general junk), Portobello Road (near recommended B&B's, tube: Nottinghill Gate; Monday-Thursday general, Friday and Saturday flea market,
9:00-5:00), and Camden Lock (the biggest flea market on Saturdays and
Sundays, 9:00-6:00, tube: Camden Town).
▲▲▲**British Museum**—The greatest chronicle of our civilization anywhere, this immense museum can only be dipped into. Take a long
walk—like hiking through Encyclopedia Britannica National Park—then
cover just two or three sections of your choice more thoroughly. The
Egyptian, Mesopotamian, Greek (Parthenon) and Manuscripts (Magna
Carta) sections are a few of my favorites. Free, open Monday-Saturday
10:00-5:00, Sunday 2:30-6:00. (tube: Tottenham Court Road).

▲▲**Tate Gallery**—One of Europe's great houses of art, the Tate specializes in British painting (1500—contemporary, with great Turner and Blake collections) and in international modern art (Matisse, Van Gogh, Monet). Learn about the mystical watercolorist Blake and the Romantic nature-worship art of Turner. Lots of tours, a great gift shop. Free, open Monday-Saturday 10:00-6:00, Sunday 2:00-6:00. (tube: Pimlico).

▲▲**The City of London**—When Londoners say "the city," they mean the one-square-mile business, banking and journalism center that 2,000 years ago was Londinium. The outline of The Roman City Walls can still be seen in the arc of roads from Blackfriars Bridge to the Tower Bridge. Within the city are 24 churches designed by Christopher Wren.

Wren's most famous church is the great St. Paul's, with an elaborate interior capped by a 365-foot dome. St. Paul's is the symbol of British resistance, as Nazi bombs actually bounced off it in World War II. It was the wedding church of Prince Charles and Lady Di. Climb the dome for a great city view and some fun in the whispering gallery—talk into the wall and your partner on the far side can hear you. (Tours 10:00-4:15, open 9:00-6:00. Allow an hour to go up and down the dome—it's good exercise).

A place near and dear to the busy people in three-piece suits and "tightly-wrapped" umbrellas that clog that city by day is The Stock Exchange (free tours Monday-Friday, 9:45-3:30). Also worth a look is the Central Criminal Courts known as "Old Bailey". An hour in the visitors' gallery (Monday-Friday 10:15-1:00, 2:00-4:00, closed in August) is always fascinating.

▲**Museum of London**—For a great walk through London history — from pre-Roman times on. Open Tuesday-Saturday 10:00-6:00, Sunday 2:00-6:00. (tube: Barbican).

▲**Victoria and Albert Museums**—surprisingly interesting collection of costumes, armor, furniture, decorative arts, and much more. Monday-Thursday and Saturday 10:00-6:00, Sunday 2:20-5:00. Closed Friday. £2 donation asked. (Tube: So. Kensington).

Entertainment and Theater
You could spend a lifetime being entertained in London. It's bubbling with top-notch shows seven nights a week, reaching a boil each summer. The key to maximizing your entertainment pleasure is to take advantage of "What's On," "City Limits," or "Time Out," available at most newsstands. You can telephone 246-8041 for a recording of today's events. You'll choose from classical, jazz, rock and far-out music, Gilbert and Sullivan, dance, comedy, spectator sports, film and theater.

I'd focus on the theater. London's Theater rivals Broadway in quality but is much cheaper. Choose from the Royal Shakespeare Company, top musicals, comedy, thrillers, sex farces, and more. Performances are nightly except Sunday, usually with one matinee a week. Matinees (listed in a box in "What's On") are cheaper and normally not sold out.

Most theaters are in the Piccadilly-Trafalgar area, and are marked on tourist maps. Most theaters, box offices, hotels and Tourist offices have a very handy "Theater Guide" brochure listing everything in town. The quickest and easiest way to get a ticket is through a ticket agency (at Victoria T.I., or scattered throughout the theater district) but it's cheaper to go direct: call the theater, and many will hold tickets for you to be picked up an hour before show time. If it's "sold out" there's usually a way to get a seat. Call and ask how. If all else fails and money is no object, you can be victimized by a scalper.

I usually buy the second-cheapest tickets. Most theaters are so small there's hardly a bad seat. "Scooting up" later on is less than a capital offense. The famous "half price booth" in Leicester Square sells tickets the day of the show. If you'll ever enjoy Shakespeare it'll be here by the Royal Shakespeare Company in the new Barbican Centre (tel. 628-8795).

Helpful Hints
Streets are named in segments. Be on guard here more than anywhere in Britain for pickpockets and theft. You can leave anything you won't need in a well-labeled bag at your hotel since you're returning in three weeks.

Itinerary Options—Day Trips from London
London is surrounded by exciting and easy day-trip destinations. Several tour companies take London-based travelers out and back every day (call Britain Shrinkers at 629-2525 or National Express at 730-0202 or Tourist Info for ideas). The British Rail system works with London as a hub and normally offers round-trip fares that cost just a little more than their already reasonable one-way fares. See Britrail's handy "Day Trips from London" booklet. For the serious day-tripper, "Daytrips From London by Rail, Bus or Car—50 Plans" is a great guidebook (by Earl Steinbicker, Hastings House, ISBN 0803815859, $9.95)

London uses a different train station for each region. For schedule information call the appropriate station: Kings Cross—278-2477, Liverpool—283-7171, Paddington—262-6767, all others—928-5100.

DAY 3
MORE OF LONDON

After finishing up any necessary business to prepare for later in the trip, we'll continue seeing the many sights of London listed in "Day 2". There are many options depending on your interests. I'd do this:

Suggested Schedule	
8:00 am	Breakfast, easy morning, any last tour planning or telephoning. Subway to Tottenham Court Rd.
10:00 am	British Museum.
1:30 pm	Pub lunch on Fleet Street, London's frantic but dignified newspaper and print center. Or for a light healthier meal, try "Slender's Wholefood Restaurant" at 41 Cathedral Place, near St. Paul's.
2:00 pm	Walk to St. Paul's, climb to top for view. Many other Wren Churches nearby, as well as Old Bailey and the Stock Exchange.
4:00 pm	Walk to The Museum of London (open till 6:00 pm) for the best possible London history lesson.
Evening	Hopefully a performance (music or Royal Shakespeare Co.) in the new and impressive Barbican Center a block from the London Museum. (Open until 11:00 pm daily, tel. info 638-4141 ext. 218, recorded info 628-2295).

Things to do in London for your 22-day plan:
■ Reserve and pay for your hotel for your return in three weeks.
■ Reserve tickets for any special performances that are sold out now but not in three weeks (a Prom Concert in the Royal Albert Hall, tel. 589-8212, ticket to a top play like Cats, Starlight Express, Royal Shakespeare, or whatever features a big name artist).
■ Book a seat at the Stratford Theater if the RSC is playing during your Stow-on-the-Wold stay (Day 7).
■ Think ahead for Edinburgh Festival (Aug. and Sept.). Edwards and Edwards is the London ticket agency handling the festival, tel. 734-9761. (tel. 031/226-4001 in Edinburgh). If you'll hit it, reserve at least your room from London.
    Specific reservations to make (especially in July and August) for your 22-day plan:
■ B&B's in Bath, Stow, Iron Bridge and Ruthin. You may want to call any others deeper into the tour if you have a particular favorite or are ready to commit yourself to a date.
■ Ruthin Medieval Banquet—book ahead.
■ Write to Tower of London (Yeovian Warden, Tower Hill, London EC3) 3 weeks in advance, with envelope stamped and addressed to your London hotel, requesting an invitation to the moving "ceremony of the keys." Say which night or nights you can come.

DAY 4
SALISBURY, STONEHENGE, BATH

Today we pick up our car, leave the big city and tour the lively market town and cathedral of Salisbury, explore two mysterious stone circle reminders of England's ancient past—Stonehenge and Avebury—and finally get set up in the pride of Georgian England—Bath.

Suggested Schedule	
9:00	Pick up car, drive to Salisbury.
11:00	Salisbury town and cathedral. Picnic on cathedral grounds or lunch in town.
1:30	Ponder Stonehenge.
2:00	Drive to Avebury.
3:00	Don't hurry Avebury.
4:00	Lovely drive, small roads, into Bath.
5:00	Arrive, set up in Bath.

Transportation
Picking up your car. London is a terrible place to learn to drive British-style. Survivors recommend picking up your rental car out of the city at Heathrow airport. The subway or Airbus will take you there stresslessly, where major, eager rental agencies are lined up all trying harder. (If you decide to pick up your car in London, Kenning Car Hire (84 Holland Park Ave, W11, tel. 727-0123) is in "Our London Neighborhood" next to the Holland Park tube station.)

Your rental car orientation is always rushed, but be sure to understand the basics: locate the car manual, know how to change a tire, what kind of gas to use, understand their breakdown policy and how to use the AA membership (like our AAA) that comes with most car rentals. Ask the attendant for a list of drop-off offices, any map he can give you, and directions to Salisbury. Before you leave, drive around the airport parking lot and get to know your car for five or ten minutes. Note that the location of the directional signals and windshield wipers are just the opposite of US cars. Work the keys, try everything—find problems before they find you.

■ **London—Salisbury—Stonehenge (30 miles)** London, like most big cities, has a ring road, the M25. Wherever you are (airport or downtown) get on M25 and follow the "west" signs until you get to M3. M3 zips you toward Salisbury. After Basingstoke, take the A30 exit and you're 30 miles from Salisbury.

Market towns like Salisbury are parking nightmares. Follow signs to "city center" and then into a central car park.

From Salisbury, go to Amesbury via A345 where signs will get you to Stonehenge, 2 miles west.

Stonehenge has a free car park with public restrooms.

■ **Stonehenge—Avebury—Bath** Next, continue north from Amesbury on A345 to the thatched village of Upavon. "A" roads are always faster, but in this case I'd take the tiny scenic road through the villages of Hilcott, Alton Priors, and West Kennett to Avebury. You won't find a legal parking place in the village of Avebury so use the lot with the blue "P" for tourists.

From Avebury, A4 west to Calne, A3102 south to the lovely thatched village of Sandy Lane on A342. Take the tiny lane west out of Sandy Lane to the prize-winning Tudor village of Lacock. From there, take the A4 for the most beautiful approach into Bath.

If you have a road atlas book, be sure to take advantage of its city maps. In the case of Bath, navigate by bridges and landmarks. As usual, parking downtown is hopeless. Parking near your B&B shouldn't be too bad.

Sightseeing Highlights
▲▲Salisbury—Cathedral and Market—The Salisbury Cathedral, marked by the tallest spire in England, is a fine reason to stop here. Admire its exterior, the cloister, the chapter with an original Magna Carta and a ring of sculpted Old Testament scenes. See how many you can identify and then ask a guard for a sheet of "answers."

Spend some time wandering through the old center of town, particularly fun on market day (Saturday). We did our market chores here buying a "brelle" (umbrella) for $3, a sweater ($20) for the nippy and wet weather, and a few cassettes for our car tape deck.

▲▲Stonehenge—England's most famous stone circle, built 4,000 years ago in the days of Egypt's pyramids. These huge stones were brought all the way from Wales to form a remarkably accurate celestial calendar. Even today, every summer solstice (around June 21) the sun sets in just the right slot and Druids go wild. The monument is roped off so even if you pay the pound entry fee you're kept at a distance. While you can see it free from the road, it's worth a closer look.

▲▲Avebury—The stone circle at Avebury is bigger, less touristy, and I think more interesting than Stonehenge. You're free to wander among 100 stones, ditches, mounds and curious patterns from the past, as well as the village of Avebury which grew up in the middle of this 1400-foot wide Neolithic circle. Fascinating!

Itinerary Options
Speed demons could check out Winchester, a pleasant town with a great cathedral, en route to Salisbury (40 minutes extra road time). Also, if unable to spend a day for Wells and Glastonbury later, and if you're thoroughly reserved for a room in Bath, you could skip Avebury and go from Stonehenge to Glastonbury (see the Abbey, climb the tower) and on to Wells (park in the central square, see old town, bishop's palace, and great cathedral).

DAY 5
BATH

Bath is Europe's most underrated city. Any tour of Britain that skips Bath stinks. Two hundred years ago this city of 80,000 was the Hollywood of Britain. If ever a city enjoyed looking in the mirror—Bath's the one. It has more "government listed" or protected historic buildings per capita than any town in England. The entire city is built of creamy warm-tone limestone called "Bath stone." Bath beams in its cover-girl complexion. An architectural chorus line, it's the triumph of Georgian style. Bath's narcissism is justified.

Suggested Schedule	
8:15	Breakfast.
9:00	Roman baths. Double check walking tour departure time posted outside. Buy discounted combination Baths/Costume Museum ticket. Rush the museum to catch the first (and least crowded) of the guided tours which leave every 20 minutes starting at 9:20 from the actual bath (looks like a big swimming pool). You'll have 15 minutes after the tour to go back into the museum.
10:00	Enjoy a coffee break with the music of the Pump Room string trio in the elegant Pump Room just above the museum.
10:30	Take the city walking tour (depart in front of Pump Room).
12:30	Your guide will probably finish at the Assembly Rooms. Drop in to find out when the Costume guided tours leave and browse your way downhill into the old shopping center to find lunch. The Royal Victoria Park nearby is ideal picnic terrain.
3:00	Tour #1 Royal Crescent Museum.
4:00	Tour the Costume Museum in the Assembly Rooms. (Adjust your afternoon schedule to make the guided tour here. The last tour is normally at 4:30).

Sightseeing Highlights
▲▲▲The Baths—Roman and Medieval—For 2,000 years high society has enjoyed the mineral springs at Bath. Londoners traveled to "Acquae Sulis" so often to "take a bath" that finally the city became known as, simply, Bath. This hot water source of Bath's greatness is a fine Roman museum with tours every 20 minutes. Only with the enthusiastic help of your guide will the complex of ancient Roman, medieval, and modern baths and buildings make sense. Buy the combo Baths/Costume ticket here for a discount. Open 9:00-6:00 daily. Tours leave at 9:20, 9:40, 10:00 and so on throughout the day.
▲Pump Room—Just above the Roman baths, this elegant Georgian Hall is a visitor's best chance to be Old World elegant. Drop by for

morning coffee 10:00-12:00 with a string trio, or afternoon tea 3:00-5:00 with piano entertainment. This is your opportunity to have a famous but not especially good "Bath bun" and drink the curative water. ▲▲▲**Walking Tour of Bath**—These leave from the front of the Pump Room daily at 10:30 (afternoon tours as well in July and August). They are given free by local citizens who simply want to share their love of Bath with its many visitors. For a private (not free) guide call 61977, or 312901.

▲▲▲**Costume Museum** in the Assembly Room—One of Europe's great museums displaying 300 years of fashion one frilly decade at a time. Free tours leave several times a day and the guides are great. Drop by or call to check tour times. Learn why Yankee Doodle "stuck a feather in his cap and called it macaroni," and much more. Open 9:30-6:00, telephone (0225)61111.

▲▲**Royal Crescent** and **The Circus**—Bath is an architectural chorus line and these are the stars. These first elegant Georgian "condos" by John Nash are well covered in the city walking tours. The corner house at **#1 Royal Crescent**, is your best look into a house from Jane Austin's day. Expensive at £2 but worthwhile to get behind all those classy exteriors. T-S 11:00-5:00, Sun 2:00-5:00, March-October only (closed Mondays).

National Centre of Photography—The only museum of its kind I've seen, exhibiting the earliest cameras and photos and their development along with temporary contemporary exhibits. 11:00-5:30 daily except Sunday off-season.

▲**American Museum**—For years I shied away from this place. I figured I needed it like I needed a Big Mac. Upon the insistance of a friend I went, and it's great—like nothing I've seen at home. Eighteen completely furnished rooms from the 1600s to the 1800s with a guide in each room eager to fill you in on the candles, maps, bed pans, and various religious sects that make domestic Yankee history surprisingly interesting. One room is a quilter's nirvana. Open 2:00-5:00, April through October. Closed Mondays.

The Abbey—On the main square, this is worth a look. The Abbey is 500 years old, has good fan vaulting, and is most impressive during an evensong service, (schedule on the door).

Food and Accommodations
While it's one of England's most popular cities, Bath handles its crowds well. For 60p the tourist information will find you a £7 to £10 B&B. Midday arrivals should find a room but this is a place where I would call ahead—especially in peak season.

   Brock's Guest House—If you can afford the splurge, this place is the "cherry on the top" of your Bath visit. Marion Dodd just redid this home built in 1765 by John Nash. It's quiet, friendly, and couldn't be better located between the Royal Crescent and the elegant Circle at 32 Brock St. Marion charges £12 per person, with tea whenever you like, and a royal breakfast. TV in the room, laundromat around the corner. Tel. (0225)338374. Like nearly every listing in this book, she'll hold telephone reservations with no deposit until 5:00 (call if you'll be a little late).

The Georgian Guest House—Run by Sybil Barry, this place is quiet, clean, very central, friendly and—for Bath—reasonable with B&B at £10 each. The rooms are nothing special and it's one of those tall skinny places—lots of stairs. Tel. 24103. 34 Henrietta St., Bath, BA2 6LR.

For the cheapest beds, the **Youth Hostel**, tel. 65674, is very nice but not central. The **YMCA**, tel. 60471, is a bit grungy but friendly and wonderfully central on Broad St. Doubles are £6 per person, the dorm is cheaper.

Eating in Bath is fun. There's no shortage of places in all price ranges—just stroll around the center of town. I've enjoyed many meals in Bath simply by strolling until I found a place that tickled that evening's fancy. For lunch, try the cafe upstairs in the **Bartlett Street Antique Centre** (downhill from the Assembly Rooms), or the **Crystal Palace Pub** with hearty meals under rustic timbers or in the sunny courtyard (just south of the Abbey. Ask around—it's a local hangout).

Helpful Hints

The Pulteney Bridge and riverside parks are another pleasant aspect of Bath. Don't take the cleverly advertised but disappointing ghost walk. There's great shopping between the Abbey and the Assembly Rooms, especially the many antique shops. The "walk and ride" tours are not as good as the free city walks. When in need, the Pump Room's toilets are always nearby and open to the discreet public. Shops close at 5:30 except on Thursdays when they stay open later.

DAY 6
SIDE TRIP FROM BATH—WELLS, GLASTONBURY, WOOKEY HOLE

Today, after a free morning in Bath, we swing south visiting Wells, England's smallest cathedral city; Glastonbury, steeped in legends of the Holy Grail and King Arthur; and the impressive—if a bit silly—haunted caves of Wookey Hole.

Suggested Schedule

Morning	Free in Bath.
1:00	Drive to Wookey Hole.
1:30	Tour Wookey Hole.
4:00	Browse around Wells town and cathedral, staying for the 5:15 evensong service.
6:00	Drive 5 miles to Glastonbury. Tour the Abbey, then climb the tower before sun sets. Great view and eerie feelings.
8:00	Drive back to Bath, possibly stopping at a countryside pub for dinner.

Transportation

This plan calls for 50 miles of driving. The roads are good, the scenery okay but not earthshaking. I'd stick to the faster "A" roads going as direct as possible.

In Wells, try to park on the main square next to the tourist office, post office, and just about everything else. In Glastonbury, the abbey parking lot is easy to find.

Sightseeing Highlights

▲**Wookey Hole**—This is definitely a commercial venture. It's a bit tacky but I thought worth the £2.65 admission for two hours of fun. Just 2 miles from Wells, Wookey Hole is a hodgepodge of entertainment starting with a wonderfully guided tour of some big but mediocre caves complete with history, geology lessons and witch stories. Then you're free to wander through a traditional rag-paper-making mill with a demonstration, and into a 19th century circus room—a riot of color, funny mirrors and a roomful of old penny arcade machines that visitors can actually play for as long as their pennies (on sale there) last. They even have old girlie shows. Finally you come to Madame Toussaud's warehouse where the now too-young face of Prince Charles and formerly-famous faces of people like Twiggy are stored waiting for I don't know what.

▲▲**Wells**—This wonderfully preserved little cathedral city—England's smallest —is worth a stop. Its 13th century cathedral complex is one of the most interesting in England. Don't miss the carving on the west front, the unique hourglass-shaped double arch, the grand chapter house, or the nearby bishop's palace. The cathedral has a good shop and a handy cafeteria. Weekdays at 5:15 the cathedral choir gives a lovely evensong service.

If you're in the mood for a picnic, drop by the aromatic Cheese Board on the market square for a great selection of tasty local cheeses. Remember, Cheddar is just down the road. I asked the lady for the most interesting mix worth a pound.

▲▲**Glastonbury**—This place bubbles with legend and history. Its once grand and now ruined abbey is the supposed birthplace of Christianity in England. 500 years ago it was England's leading abbey. It's well worth a wander. The little abbey museum has an impressive reconstruction of the abbey as it was before Henry VIII got to it. The Glastonbury Tor (or tower) sits on a conical hill, supposedly the mystical Isle of Avalon, from King Arthur's day. You can drive around the hill and park very close to its base. Hike to the summit for a marvelous view and a great "king of the mountain" feeling. The abbey is open daily until 7:30 and the tower never closes.

Itinerary Options

If you want to see the American Museum, near Bath, which is only open from 2:00-5:00pm, skip your free time in Bath and the evensong service in Wells, doing Glastonbury first, then Wells and Wookey Hole, arriving in Claverton, outside of Bath by 3:00 to see the American Museum. Or you could follow the original schedule but replace Wookey Hole with the American Museum, getting there right at 2:00.

Wells is so pleasant you may decide to spend the night. **The Tor Guest House** on Tor Street facing the east end of the cathedral is a good value (£9, cozy lounge and breakfast room, quiet, friendly, with car park, tel. 72322). The nearby **Fountain Inn**, on St. Thomas St., is the best place for pub grub (fine curry, spare ribs and draft cider).

DAY 7
SOUTH WALES, FOLK MUSEUM, WYE RIVER VALLEY

From Bath we'll dash into South Wales for a look at its capital city of Cardiff, before spending several hours exploring the past at St. Fagan's Welsh Open-Air Folk Museum. Then we'll take the scenic route past the romantic Tintern Abbey ruins, up the lush Wye River Valley, through the remote Forest of Dean and into England's land of quaint—the Cotswold Hills—establishing our headquarters in the central village of Stow-on-the-Wold.

Suggested Schedule	
8:00	Breakfast.
8:30	Drive to Cardiff.
10:00	St. Fagan's Welsh Folk Museum. Tour grounds first, picnic, or lunch in cafeteria, then tour museum gallery.
1:00	Drive to Tintern Abbey.
2:00	Explore Tintern, Wye River, Forest of Dean.
5:00	Drive to Stow-on-the-Wold.
6:30	Set up in Stow.

Transportation
Bath—Cardiff, St. Fagan's—From Bath it's 10 miles north on A46 past a little village called Philadelphia to the M4 super freeway. Now only a speed reader can follow the map as you can go as fast as your car and conscience will let you. Crossing a huge suspension bridge you enter Wales. 20 miles later you're in Cardiff.

Follow M48, then A48, then the signs right into the center of town. You'll pass big impressive government administrative buildings, and the huge old castle that dominates the heart of Wales' biggest city. After crossing the bridge, turn right on Cathedral Road (A4119) and follow the signs 4 miles further west to St. Fagan's. If you lose the trail just ask for directions.

Cardiff—Stow—From St. Fagan's get back on the M4 as soon as possible and backtrack until just before the big suspension bridge. Take the Chepstow exit and follow the signs up A466 to Tintern Abbey and the Wye River Valley. If you stop at the Tintern Abbey, buy the Wye River-Cotswold Hills map. Carry on to Monmouth, and if you're running late follow the A40 and the M50 to the Tewkesbury exit where the A438 and the B4077 will zip you right in to Stow-on-the-Wold.

If you have time and energy, explore the romantic old Forest of Dean leaving the A466 for Coleford following the green shaded "scenic routes" through the beloved old oak forest that made Admiral Nelson's ships so strong. From Cinderford take the A48 and A40 through Cheltenham to Northleach where it's a straight ten-minute shot on A429 to Stow.

Sightseeing Highlights

Cardiff—The Welsh capital with 300,000 people and a pleasant modern center across from the castle. The castle is worthless unless you catch one of the fun tours which leave every half hour. The interior is a Victorian fantasy.

▲▲▲**St. Fagan's Welsh Folk Museum**—This is your best look at traditional Welsh folk life. Twenty old houses from all corners of this little country have been saved and reconstructed here. Each is fully furnished with a local expert warming herself by the toasty fire and happy to tell you anything you want to know about life in this old cottage. You'll also see traditional crafts in action and a fascinating gallery displaying crude washing machines, the earliest matches, elaborately carved "love spoons" and even a case of memorabilia from the local man who pioneered cremation. Everything is well explained. The cafeteria is pleasant and cheap, a good lunch option. Museum admission is 2£. Open daily 10:00-5:00, Sundays 2:30-5:00.

▲**Caerphilly Castle**—A very impressive but gutted old castle, only thirty minutes from St. Fagan's. The second largest in Europe after Windsor, it has two concentric walls and was considered to be a brilliant arrangement of defensive walls and moats. It's interesting to see how Cromwell's demolition crew tried to destroy it, creating the leaning tower of Caerphilly. Open daily 9:30-6:30. (Note: this 22-day tour covers other equally impressive fortresses, so you may want to skip this one to make time for the scenic drive to Stow.)

▲**Tintern Abbey**—Just off the scenic A466 road in a lush natural setting, this is worth a stop. The abbey shop and local tourist information desk next door are very helpful. You can buy the Wye-Cotswolds map and "A Tourist Guide to North Wales" here.

▲**Wye River Valley** and **Forest of Dean**—Lush, mellow and historic, this region seduced me into an unexpected overnight. Read up on the Forest of Dean with its special dialect, strange political autonomy and its ties to Trafalgar and Admiral Nelson.

Food and Accommodations—Stow-on-the-Wold

Stow-on-the-Wold is the ideal homebase for the Cotswolds. While it has its crowds, most are day-trippers and even summer nights are peaceful. Stow has plenty of B&B options and a tourist office on the main square that can get you set up. Here are some specifics.

The Stow-Away B&B—Norman and Barbara Axon make you feel like part of the family. Only after an hour of tea and talk did I have a chance to actually bring in my bag. Just opened in 1985, they are two blocks off the main square (14 Park St., Stow-on-the-Wold, Gloucestershire, tel. 31839, £8 B&B, with tea in the evening). Take the loft room if you can.

Kent House—Another pleasant place, centrally located on Sheep Street (three doors from the post office), run by Patricia and Dennis Burnford (and dog Susie), tel. 30387.

The Guest House—6 miles west of Stow in the tiny village of Guiting Power, this is your sleepy village alternative. Modern, clean, and friendly, in a 400-year-old house. £9, Post Office Lane, Guiting Power, Cheltenham, GL545T2, tel. (04515) 470.

Stow-on-the-Wold Youth Hostel—Right on the main square of Stow in an historic old building, well run, friendly atmosphere, good food served or do-it-yourself in member's kitchen, two double rooms for married hostellers, popular in summer. Call in reservations at (0451) 30497. £3 per night.

Other Cotswold Youth Hostels—The hostels at Cleve Hill (tel. (024267) 2065, Duntisbourne Abbots (tel. (028582) 682), and Charlburg (tel. (0608) 810202) are good bases for exploring the Cotswold villages. They are special because they rent bikes for £2 per day. Call (05432) 22279 for specifics.

Pub Grub—Have dinner at the **Queen's Head** on the main square. Try their local Cotswold brew, Donnington.

Itinerary Options

If you want to skip the scenic three hours of Tintern, Wye, and Dean, you could spend an hour in Cardiff and an hour at the Caerphilly Castle, and take the Motorway (M4, M5) and A436 direct to Stow. Or, if you stepped up the tempo throughout, adding just a tinge of hecticity to the plan, you could sneak Caerphilly Castle into the suggested itinerary after St. Fagan's.

For a special night check into the **St. Briavals Castle Youth Hostel** (tel. (0594) 530272, closed Sundays, £3, you must be a Youth Hostel member). It's an 800-year-old Norman Castle, used by King John, comfortable (as far as castles go), friendly, and in the center of the quiet village of St. Griavels just north of Tintern Abbey. For dinner, eat at the hostel or walk "just down the path and up the snyket" to the **Crown Pub** (very friendly, with good cheap food and fine pub atmosphere).

DAY 8
THE COTSWOLD VILLAGES AND BLENHEIM PALACE

Today we mix England's coziest villages with her greatest countryside palace. The Cotswold Hills are dotted with storybook villages and the best are within easy reach of Stow-on-the-Wold. England has plenty of royal country mansions. If you had to choose just one to visit (and we do) Blenheim is it.

Suggested Schedule

8:00	Breakfast in Stow-on-the-Wold.
8:30	Drive to Chipping Campden.
9:00	Joyride through Chipping Campden, Broadway, and Stanton, drive via Cheltenham to Cirencester (park in central lot).
11:00	Cirencester—Corinium Museum, crafts center, lunch in crafts center cafeteria.
1:00	Drive to Bibury via Coln St. Dennis, Coln Rogers, and Winson.
1:30	Bibury—stroll the stream, cottages, church.
2:30	Drive to Blenheim via Burford, Witney, and Woodstock (A4095).
3:15	Park at palace and line up for the hour tour of Blenheim Palace.
5:15	Drive to Stow-on-the-Wold via Chipping Norton.
6:00	Evening stroll around Stow center, find a good pub for dinner.

The Cotswolds
Like many fairytale regions of Europe, the present day beauty of the Cotswolds is explained by economic ups and downs. The area grew rich on the wool trade and built lovely towns and houses. Then foreign markets stole their trade and they slumped—too poor even to be knocked down. The forgotten time-passed villages have now been discovered by us 20th-century romantics, and the Cotswold villages are enjoying a new prosperity.

Transportation
While distances are very small in the Cotswolds, so are the roads. Including the 20-mile drive to Blenheim, we'll probably put in 100 miles today—most of it as joyful as joyriding can be. Don't bumble around without a good map—any shop can sell you a fine tourist-oriented map of the region. No Cotswold town is big enough to cause any problems except for peak season parking in Broadway and Bourton. Blenheim Palace is in the town of Woodstock on A34, 7 miles northwest of Oxford. The palace turnoff is right in the town, not well signposted. By the way, a "quick swing into Oxford" won't work—it has the worst traffic

and parking problems in England. Today's theme is to take the tiny
roads.

Sightseeing Highlights

▲**Stow-on-the-Wold**—Eight roads converge on Stow but none inter-
rupt the peacefulness of its main square. The town has no real sights
other than itself. There are several good pubs, some pleasant shops and
a handy little walking tour brochure called "Town Trail" (15p, sold at
Youth Hostel counter). Put yourself in the stocks on the green and
ponder our saying "he was the laughing stock of the town."

▲**Cirencester**—1800 years ago, this was the ancient Roman city,
Corinium. It's found 20 miles from Stow down A429 or, in Roman
times, down Foss Way. In Cirencester don't miss the Corinium Museum
(open 10:00-6:00, Sundays 2:00-6:00) to find out why they say "if you
scratch Gloucestershire you'll find Rome." The craft center and work-
shops entertain visitors with traditional weaving, baking, potting, etc. in
action. There's also an interesting gallery and a great cafeteria. Friday is
market day in Cirencester.

Cotswold Farming and Prison Museum—9 miles south of Stow, just
off the Foss Way (A429) at Northleach. Worthwhile if you're interested
in old farming machines (no crowd problems. . .ever).

Bourton-on-the-Water—4 miles south of Stow. I can't figure out if
they call this the "Venice of the Cotswolds" because of its quaint canals,
its miserable crowds, or just to make more money. It's too cute, worth a
drive through but no more.

Broadway—9 miles northwest of Stow. Another very crowded town,
worth a drive-through but not a stop. . .there won't be a parking place
anyway.

▲**Chipping Campden**—9 miles north of Stow. This is a close second
to Stow for the best homebase. A real working market town, home of
some incredibly beautiful thatched roofs and the richest Cotswold wool
merchants ("Cotswold" comes from the Saxon phrase "hills of sheeps
coats"). Pleasant for a walk.

▲▲**Snowshill** and **Stanton**—Both 2 miles south of Broadway. These
two towns, along with Upper and Lower Slaughter (3 miles south of
Stow) are my nominations for the most lovely Cotswold villages.
They're so cute you can almost eat them (but don't). All are nestled in
equally beautiful countryside.

▲**Bibury**—6 miles northeast of Cirencester. This is an entertaining
town with a trout farm, Cotswolds museum, stream thriving with huge
trout and proud ducks, a row of very old weavers' cottages, and a
church surrounded by rose trees—each tended by a volunteer of the
parish. Don't miss the scenic drive from Bibury to A429 through the villages of Winson, Coln St. Dennis and Coln Rogers.

▲▲▲**Blenheim Palace**—It's easy to O.D. on English palaces, so this
tour chooses just the best. The Duke of Marlborough's home is still
lived in, which is wonderfully obvious as you tour it. Churchill was
born prematurely while his mother was at a Blenheim Palace party
(Truly a man before his time). The palace is well organized; only tours
are allowed in. They leave every ten minutes, last an hour, cost £3.
There's an excellent new Churchill exhibit which is worth lingering

over, so skip to the next tour group if you need more time here. The palace is open from March through October, 11:00-6:00, last tour leaves at 5:00.

Itinerary Options
For a more leisurely day, skip Chipping Campden and Broadway and check out Upper and Lower Slaughter and Bourton-on-the-Water as you drive down to Cirencester. You could drive through Chipping Campden and Broadway on your way to Stratford tomorrow morning.

Remember, you're just 30 miles from Stratford, Shakespeare's birthplace. The world's best Shakespeare is performed by the Royal Shakespeare Company there and in London. You'll need to get your tickets in advance (in London on the first day of your trip), but if you're a Shakespeare fan, it's worth the trouble.

If you'd prefer Oxford to Cambridge (which is reasonable even if I don't), you can do it as a side trip from London or from Stow-on-the-Wold. Consider an extra day in the itinerary here which would give you a whole day in the Cotswolds and a day split between Blenheim and Oxford (11:00 Blenheim tour, in Oxford by 1:00, get straight to the tourist office to reserve a spot on an afternoon city walking tour).

DAY 9

STRATFORD UPON AVON, WARWICK CASTLE, AND COVENTRY CATHEDRAL TO IRON BRIDGE GORGE

Today we travel north into the cradle of the Industrial Revolution stopping en route at Shakespeare's birthplace in Stratford. We'll also tour England's greatest medieval castle in Warwick and visit Coventry and its cathedral, the symbol of the destruction of World War II, the determination to rebuild and the hope for peace and reconciliation. Then we zoom (hopefully) through England's second largest city, Birmingham, and into the valley of the Severn River, once churning with industry and now a land of sleepy smokestacks, soothing natural beauty and a distinct Shropshire brand of hospitality.

Suggested Schedule	
8:30 am	Leave Stow-on the-Wold.
9:15 am	Park in Stratford.
9:30 am	See the "World of Shakespeare" show.
10:00 am	Walk around town, visit Shakespeare house.
12:00	Drive to Warwick (picnic in car or leave Stratford early and lunch at the castle).
12:30 pm	Tour castle.
2:30 pm	Drive to Coventry.
2:45 pm	Tour new and old Cathedral, visitor's center, and wander around Coventry.
5:00 pm	Drive to Iron Bridge Gorge.
6:30 pm	Arrive in Iron Bridge Gorge.

Transportation

Today's sights are close together and served by fine roads. There's no joyriding in this plan, as we'll drive directly from each stop to the next. From Stow, drive 20 miles north on A429 and A34 to Stratford. In Stratford cross the bridge and you're in the center. Take the immediate left and park as close to the big modern theater as you can.

It's only 8 miles to Warwick along A46. The castle is well signposted, just south of town to the right of the main road.

After Warwick, follow the signs to Coventry (still on A46), and in Coventry follow signs to "city centre" and then to "cathedral." The cathedral is hard to see so just look for signs. When you get to what looks like a large bus station, park in the highrise "cathedral car park."

From the cathedral follow signs through lots of sprawl to the M6 and you're on your way. The M6 will take you right through giant Birmingham. Our plan takes you through during rush hour but it doesn't seem to be a problem. From M6 take the new M54 to the Telford/Iron Bridge exit. Iron Bridge signs will take you through a long series of roundabouts until you're there.

Cotswolds to Iron Bridge

SHREWSBURY
TELFORD
IRONBRIDGE
M 54
BIRMINGHAM
M 6
COVENTRY
WARWICK
STRATFORD ON AVON
M 5
STOW
CHELTENHAM
COTSWOLDS
BLENHEIM
CIRENCESTER
OXFORD

0   10   20
MILES

Sightseeing Highlights
Stratford upon the Avon—This is the most overrated tourist magnet
in England, but we're passing through, and nobody back home would
understand if we skipped Shakespeare's house.

Shakespeare's hometown is blanketed with opportunities for "bardol-
otry." Only his birthplace on Henley Street is worth a visit on our
itinerary. You'll enter through a modern "Shakespeare Center" which
has little to offer besides some fine BBC theater costumes, clean toilets
and a high-tech cash register which from 9:00-6:00 daily will relieve
you of £1.70.

"The World of Shakespeare" shows (25 minutes, £1.75) go on the
half-hour, located between the big Theater and the bridge.

▲▲**Royal Shakespeare Company**—The RSC is undoubtedly the best
Shakespeare Company on earth. They split their season between
London and Stratford. If you're a Shakespeare fan, see if the RSC
schedule works into your itinerary while you're in London at the start
of your trip. It's easy to make a Stratford show from Stow-on-the-Wold,
or in London before you fly home. You will need to buy your tickets in
advance.

▲▲▲**Warwick Castle**—England's finest medieval castle is well organized to give its hordes of visitors a good value for the steep £3.25
entry fee. Situated above the Avon River with a lush green grassy moat

and fairytale fortification, Warwick will entertain you from dungeon to lookout. There's something for every taste—a fine and educational armory, a terrible torture chamber, a knight in shining armor posing on a horse, a Madame Tussaud re-creation of a royal weekend party—an 1898 game of statue-maker—and a grand garden and park patrolled by peacocks that's ideal for a picnic.

▲▲**Coventry's Cathedral**—The Germans bombed Coventry to smithereens in 1940. From that point on their word for "to really blast the heck out of a place" was to "coventrate". But Coventry left smithereens, and its message to our world is one of forgiveness and reconciliation. The symbol of Coventry is the bombed out hulk of its old cathedral with the brilliant new one adjoining it. The complex is designed for visitors. Climb the tower, pick up a guided walk brochure, savour the powerful modern art, search for the symbolism, ask a hostess about the "Community of the Cross of Nails," see the Visitors Center (£1.25 donation to the church, daily 9:30-6:00, Sunday 12:00-6:00) with its award-winning 18-minute movie "The Spirit of Coventry." Have tea and scones in the cafeteria.

Accommodations

The Iron Bridge Gorge is a young attraction and doesn't have a lot of accommodations, but these are good:

   The Tontine Hotel—Centrally located, exactly across from the Iron Bridge itself. It's old (1784), brick, historic, and a bit musty—in keeping with the style of the valley. For £12 each you'll get a very nice room, traditional breakfast, hotel-type service, and a helpful management happy to give sightseeing advice (tel. 2127).

   The Hill View Farm—Mrs. Hawkins runs a peaceful, clean, and friendly farmhouse B&B in a great rural setting overlooking the ruins of an old Abbey. A real value for £7½. Address: Buildwas, Iron Bridge, Shropshire; tel. 2228. Located halfway between Iron Bridge and Much Wenlock—leave Iron Bridge past the huge modern power plants (coal, not nuclear, but ominous nonetheless), cross the bridge and go about a mile. You'll see the sign.

   Wilderhope Manor Youth Hostel—The beautifully remote and haunted 500-year-old manor house is one of my favorite youth hostels anywhere in Europe. One day a week tourists actually pay to see what we youth hostelers sleep in for £3. Six and a half miles from Much Wenlock down B4371 towards Church Stretton. Tel (06943) 363. Evening meal served at 7:00 pm.

   Iron Bridge Gorge Youth Hostel—Built in 1859 as the Coalbrookdale Institute, this grand hostel is a 20-minute walk from the Iron Bridge, down A4169 towards Wellington. Tel. (095245) 3281.

   Other B&Bs in Iron Bridge Gorge: Mrs. Roberts (Woodland Grange, 48 Lincoln Hill, tel. 2309), Mrs. Bowdler (Vine Cottage, 45 Lincoln Hill, tel. 3767), Mrs. Pearce (The Grove, New Road, tel. 3218), Mrs. Gilbride (Paradise House, Coalbrookdale, 3379), Mrs. Heath (Coalbrookdale Villa, Paradise, Coalbrookdale, tel. 3450), Mrs. Tyley (Wren's Nest Cottage, 45 Newbridge Road, tel. 3061).

DAY 10
IRON BRIDGE
GORGE MUSEUMS—NORTH WALES

Today we'll go from the gritty pits of England's industrial infancy to the poetic hills of remote northern Wales. The Industrial Revolution started in England's Severn River Valley. Today this area is preserved as a showcase of the days that boosted England into world leadership.

Suggested Schedule	
8:30 am	Breakfast.
9:30 am	Iron Bridge, town, shops.
10:00 am	Severn Warehouse, intro video, exhibit.
11:00 am	Museum of Iron, Darby's furnace, "Rosehill," Darby's House.
12:00	Blist's Hill Museums, picnic, cafeteria or pub lunch.
3:30 pm	Drive to Wales.
4:30 pm	Llangollen, 30-minute stop in town or at abbey.
5:00 pm	Horseshoe Pass Road to Ruthin.
6:00 pm	Check in the Ruthin B&B.
7:30 pm	Medieval Banquet at Ruthin Castle.
11:00 pm	Find your way home.
12:00 am	Still not home? More mead!

Iron Bridge Gorge
In its glory days this now-sleepy valley gave the world the first iron wheels, trains, cast iron bridge and steam locomotives and powered Britain to the pinnacle of the industrial world.

Sightseeing Highlights
▲▲▲**Iron Bridge Gorge Industrial Revolution Museums**—
  Start with *the* Iron Bridge. The first ever (1779), this is the area's centerpiece, open all the time and free.
  The Severn Warehouse 200 yards up stream is the orientation center. Be here at 10:00 when it opens to see the intro movie, check out its exhibit, buy your guidebook and tickets (£3.50 for the whole area).
  Just up the road in Coalbrookdale is the Museum of Iron (worth a quick look), Darby's first blast furnace and his house, "Rosehill." It was here, in 1709, that Abraham Darby first smelted iron using coke as fuel. If you're like me, "coke" is a drink and "smelt" is the past tense of smell, but this event kicked off the modern industrial age.
  Save most of your time and energy for the great Blist's Hill Open Air Museum—50 acres of Victorian industry, factories, and a recreated community from the 1890s complete with shoe makers, ancient dentist's chair, candle makers, a working pub, a fascinating squatter's cottage and a noisy slip-slidey pigsty. Take the lovely walk along the canal to the inclined plane, have a picnic or visit the cafeteria near the squatter's cottage. Buy the guidebook for a good step-by-step rundown. Open 10:00-6:00 daily. Info tel. (095245)3522, or 3418 on weekends.

Iron Bridge

TO SHREWSBURY, WALES
TO TELFORD, M 54, M 6
ROSE HILL, DARBY'S HOUSE
MUSEUM OF IRON
COALBROOKDALE
YOUTH HOSTEL
IRON BRIDGE TOWER
BLIST'S HILL OPEN-AIR MUSEUM
MUCH WENLOCK FARM VIEW B & B
SEVERN RIVER
SEVERN RIVER
SEVERN WAREHOUSE TOURIST INFO, ORIENTATION
IRON BRIDGE

Transportation—Iron Bridge to Wales

Most of the day is spent at easy-to-find museums within a few miles of the Iron Bridge. In mid-afternoon we'll drive for an hour to Wales via A458 through Shrewsbury, crossing the border at the cute castletown of Chirk. There take A5 to Llangollen. Cross the bridge in Llangollen, turn left and follow A542 and A525 past the romantic Valle Crucis Abbey, over the scenic Horseshoe Pass, and into Ruthin.

Sightseeing Highlights—North Wales

Llangollen—Well worth a stop, Llangollen is famous for its International Eisteddfod (July 1-10), a festival of folk songs and dance, very popular—and crowded. You can walk or ride a horse-drawn boat down its old canal towards the lovely 13th-century Cistercian Abbey near the even older and more thought-provoking old cross called Eliseg's Pillar. You'll at least glimpse all these things from the A542 on your way up the exciting Horseshoe Pass.

Ruthin—The ideal home base for your exploration of North Wales. Ruthin (pron: Rithin) is a market town serving the scenic Vale of Clwyd (pron: Klide). Each Wednesday is Medieval Day (pron: day) as the square dresses up and everything goes traditional (10:00-5:00 in summer). The Tourist Info Office (10:00-5:00 daily, tel. (08242)3992) can give you plenty of info and book reservations for rooms and the medieval banquet. Located in a busy crafts center with 14 working shops, a gallery and a fine cafeteria, the place bubbles with small town community spirit.

▲▲**The Ruthin Castle Medieval Banquet**—By most accounts, this is Britain's best "medieval banquet." Of course, it's a touristy gimmick— but what a *fun* one. For one crazy evening I chose to accept this romanticized trip into the bawdy Welsh past. English, Scottish, Irish and Welsh medieval banquets are all variations on the same theme. This one is more tasteful and less expensive than most—and it plays right into our 22-day plan.

You'll start off with a chunk of bread dipped in salt which the maiden mentions will "guarantee your safety." Your medieval master of ceremonies then seats you and the evening of food, drink, and music rolls gaily on. Harp music, angelic singing, mead, spiced wine, four hearty traditional courses eaten with your fingers and a dagger, bibs, candle light, pewter goblets and lots of entertainment including insults slung at the Irish, Scots, English and even us brash colonists.

These banquets cost £13.50, start at 7:30 nearly every evening and usually sell out (well in advance on Friday and Saturday evenings). Call in a reservation at (08242)3435. The castle is just down Castle Street from the town square, easy parking at the doorstep.

Accommodations

Cilgwyn is an elegant old house run by busy Mrs. Hunter (who also has a big shop on the main square). The place has a view, a comfy lounge, fine breakfasts and a classy but make-yourself-at-home atmosphere. On Greenfield Road, the first left in the direction of "Mold" past the Tourist Information and craft center—just a 5-minute walk from T.I. and 10 minutes from the town square and castle. Tel. 4486. £9.

   Hendre is just before you get to Cilgwyn, also on Greenfield Road. Mr. & Mrs. King run this place in a way that makes you part of the family immediately. Mr. King is happy to help with sightseeing ideas. The house is small, modern, clean. TV's in each room. £9. Tel. 4078.

The Wine Vaults is an old inn right on Ruthin's main square. Run by Mrs. Taylor, pub downstairs, most central possible location, great guests-'lounge, modern plumbing. A little musty and less cozy than a B&B. Tel. 2067, £10.

The Ruthin Castle is the ultimate in old world elegance for North Wales. It's worth the £25. they charge for B&B. Tel. (08242) 2664.

Hiker's Hostel **Nant-yr-Hafod**. This is a simple stone cottage just off the ancient Offa's Dyke Path. Not an official youth hostel, just a handy £3 bed for budget travelers. Two dorms and a double, ½ mile off A525, 6 miles before Ruthin, turn at Plough Inn. Address: Hafod Bilston, Llandegla Wrexham, Clwyd, tel (097888) 693.

McGregor's Pit B&B—If you don't mind unflushed toilets, dog hairs everywhere, an occasional old tampon in the corner and windows boarded shut, call this place. Mr. McGregor keeps his house too warm but serves a cold breakfast and usually wants payment in advance. (£14. No telephone or address)

Food
Pub Grub—The **White Horse Inn** in the village of Llanfair, 2 miles out of Ruthin on A525 has great food and a friendly atmosphere, well-stocked with Welsh friends, fun pool-and-darts room. Jimmy runs the place spending more time mingling than behind the bar. He laughs like a billy goat or sheep trying to get your attention.

Itinerary Options
If you're not into heavy metal, leave the Iron Bridge museums early after lunch (skip the Museum of Iron, doing just the Blist's Hill Museum) and take a scenic detour from Iron Bridge south along Wenlock Edge (B4368) for the best Shropshire scenery. Use the 95p Shropshire guide available at any local tourist office. Drive from Clun, wind up to Welshpool and from there to Llangollen for a longer stop.

Also, if you can't do the medieval banquet tonight, try to book it for tomorrow. If you didn't buy the North Wales guide in South Wales, get it in Llangollen.

DAY 11
EXPLORING NORTH WALES

Variety is the spice of travel and our day includes: a tour of Caernarfon, North Wales' mightiest castle; one of the world's largest slate mines at Blaenau Ffestiniog; and some of Britain's most beautiful scenery in the Snowdonia National Park, driving around the towering Mount Snowdon through lush forests and desolate Moor country.

Suggested Schedule

8:30 am	Breakfast (earlier if possible).
9:00 am	Drive to Caernarfon with short stops in Penmachno Mill, Betws-y-Coed (info center, shops, or waterfalls), and over Llanberis Mountain Pass.
11:30 am	Arrive at Caernarfon, picnic on waterfront
12:00	Caernarfon Castle. Catch 12:00 tour, 1:00 movie in Eagle Tower, 1:30 climb to top for view.
2:00	Walk through town, shop, see Regimental Museum or Prince Charles (of Wales) Exhibit in castle.
2:30 pm	Drive scenic road to Blaenau Ffestiniog.
3:30 pm	Tour Llechwedd Slate Mines.
5:30 pm	Drive home via Denbigh.
7:00 pm	Arrive in Ruthin. Dinner (with Jimmy) in White Horse Inn in Llanfair.

Transportation

Every road in North Wales has its charm, but this day includes the best—lots of scenic joyriding on small roads. Take the little B5105 road out of Ruthin to Cerrigydrudion (down the steepest road off the main square and follow the signs to Cerrigydrudion). Then follow the A5 into Betws-y-Coed with a possible quick detour to the Penmachno Woolen Mill (one mile south on B4406, well signposted). At Chapel Curig take A4086 over the rugged Pass of Llanberis, just under the summit of Mt. Snowdon, and on to Caernarfon. Park under the castle (very central) in the harborside car park.

The A4085 from Caernarfon southeast through Beddgelert to Pen-rhyndendraeth is lovely. Make things even more beautiful by taking the little B4410 road from Garreg to Maentwrog. Go through the depressing and dark mining town of Blaenau Ffestiniog on A470 until you wind up into the hills of slate and turn right into the Llechwedd Slate Mine.

After the mine, A470 continues north into the most scenic stretch of all (several remote and intriguing B&B's if you decide to spend the night) through Dolwyddelan and back to A5 which you'll take for 6 miles east before following the windy, windy (curvey, blowey) A543 road over the stark moors to Denbigh (drive up to the castle for a fine view. From Denbigh you're a 15-minute ride to Ruthin.

Sightseeing Highlights

Betws-y-Coed—This is the resort center of the Snowdonia National Park, with more than its share of tour buses and souvenir shops. It has a good National Park and Tourist Information office. The main street is worth a walk. Two miles south of town is the Penmachno Woolen Mill—just 1 mile off A5, free, and surprisingly interesting. On the other side of town (you'll see the car park a mile down A5) is Swallow Falls. Depending on where you come from, these are also worth a linger. (5 minute walk from road.)

▲▲**Caernarfon Castle**—Edward I built this impressive castle 700 years ago to establish English rule over North Wales. It's a great castle, all ready to entertain. See the movie (on the half hour in the Eagle Tower), climb the Eagle Tower for a great view, take the guided tour (50 minutes, included in admission price, on the hour from center of courtyard in front of entry) and see the special exhibit on the investiture of Prince Charles and earlier Princes of Wales.

▲**Llechwedd Slate Mine Tour**—Slate mining played a huge role in the Welsh heritage and this mine on the north edge of the bleak mining town of Blaenau Ffestiniog does its best to explain the mining culture of Wales. This is basically a romanticized view of the depressing existence of the Welsh miners of the Victorian age who put the slate roofs on most of Europe. Wales has a poor economy, so tourist-izing slate mines is understandable. Open 10:00-6:00 daily, tours £2.15/£3.25, tel. (0766)830306.

Helpful Hints

The Welsh language is alive and well. In a pub, impress your friends (or make some) by toasting the guy who may have just bought your drink. Say "Yuchk-eh dah" (meaning "good health to you") and "Dee och" ("thank you") or "Dee och on vowr" ("thanks very much").

DAY 12
BLACKPOOL, ENGLAND'S "ATLANTIC CITY"

Today we go from God's glorious garden to Man's tacky glittering city of fun, from pristine North Wales to the bells and blinkers of Blackpool. Blackpool, a middle-sized city with a six-mile beach promenade, is ignored by guidebooks (*Let's Go: Britain* in 500 pages of small print never even mentions Blackpool), and even the most thorough bus tour will show you castles till your ears crenulate but never take an American visitor to Blackpool.

This is Britain's fun puddle where every Englishman goes—but none will admit it. It's England's most visited attraction, the private domain of its working class. When I told Brits I was Blackpool-bound, their expression soured and they asked, "Oh God, why?" Because it's the place local widows and workers go year after year to escape. Tacky, yes. Lowbrow, okay. But it's as English as can be, and that's what I'm here for.

Our plan is to enjoy a slow morning in Ruthin, drive two hours, get set up and spend the rest of the day just "muckin' about" (British for "messin' around"). If you're bored in Blackpool, you're tired of life.

Suggested Schedule	
9:00 am	Breakfast, slow morning.
10:00 am	Ruthin, free time, craft center, shopping.
11:00 am	Drive to Blackpool, picnic enroute.
1:00 pm	Blackpool. Visit tourist office (follow signs) and set up in a B&B, buy show ticket, catch a tram to the South Pier.
2:00 pm	Pleasure Beach.
4:30 pm	The Blackpool Tower.
7:30 pm	Old Time Music Hall Show.
10:00 pm	Prowl through the night lights, people, one armed bandits, pubs and clubs of England's "Atlantic City."

Transportation
You'll be amazed how fast the motorway will get you to Blackpool. From Ruthin take A494 through the town of Mold and follow the blue signs to the motorway. M56 will zip you to M6 where you'll turn north towards Preston and Lancaster. After Preston take the M55 right into Blackpool and drive as close as you can to the stubby Eiffel-type tower in their town center. From here you're a short walk to the tourist office and to the B&B district around Albert Road. Park carefully; petty vandals abound.

Sightseeing Highlights
Tourist Info Office—First of all, go to the helpful T.I. Get the city map (20p), pick up brochures from all the amusement centers, and go over your plans. Ask about special shows and evening events and for advice on rooms.

Remember, Blackpool is second only to London as a center for live theater.

▲Blackpool Tower—Much more than a tower, this is a giant fun center. You pay £2.50 to get in, and after that the fun is free. Working your way up from the bottom, check out the fascinating aquarium, the bad house of silly horrors, the very elegant ballroom with live music and dancing all day, the dance of discovery (funny mirrors and lots of hands-on curiosities—don't miss the "Meet Your Friends" chamber and the robot that will actually verbalize whatever you type). The finale is the tower. This symbol of Blackpool is a stubby version of its more famous Parisian cousin. Still, the view from the top is smashing. Consider a coffee break before leaving to watch the golden oldies dance to the grand pipe organ in the ballroom.

Tram cars—Survey Blackpool's 6-mile beach promenade from a vintage trolley car. They go up and down the waterfront constantly and make much more sense than driving.

The Gypsie Rosalee type spiritualists—a fixture at Blackpool. I was told I "mustn't leave without having my fortune told" but, at £2.50 per palm, I'll read them myself.

▲▲Old Time Music Hall Show—There are many shows at Blackpool but its specialty is the old-fashioned variety that went out with vaudeville. These are a great hit with "Twirlies" (senior citizens, infamous for using their bus passes "too-early" before rush hour fades). It's definitely a corny show—neither hip nor polished—but it's fascinating to be surrounded by hundreds of partying British seniors, swooning again, waving their hankies to the predictable beat, and giggling at jokes I'd never tell my grandma. Bus loads of happy widows come from all corners of England to enjoy an "Old Time Music Hall Show." Buy your ticket in the afternoon, about £3.50, ask a local for the best show, probably on a pier. Try for Mike Donohoe's "Great Days of Music Hall" show (he should be on the North Pier through '86).

"The Illuminations"—Every late September and October Blackpool stretches its season by "illuminating" its 6-mile waterfront with countless lights all blinking and twinkling to the delight of those who visit this electronic festival. The American in me kept saying "I've seen bigger and I've seen better" but I shut him up and just had some simple fun like everyone on my specially decorated tram.

▲Pleasure Beach—These 42 acres of rides (over 80, including "the best selection of big thrill rides in Europe"), ice skating shows, cabarets, and amusements attract six million people a year, making it England's most popular attraction.

▲▲People Watching—Blackpool's top sight is its people. You'll see England here like nowhere else. Grab someone's hand, a big stick of "candy floss" and stroll.

Accommodations

Blackpool is in the business of accommodating people who can't afford to go to Spain. Simple B&Bs and hotels abound. The classy expensive hotels are, predictably, along the waterfront. Countless lackluster budget alternatives cluster, very handy and central, around Albert Road, near the Central Pier and the tower. These B&Bs almost all have the same design—minimal character, maximum number of beds. Double rooms (in the six or seven places I visited) are all the same small size with a small double bed, your basic English breakfast and a decent shower down the hall. Prices range from £8 (dingy) to £10 (cheery) per person.

Arriving at midday, you should have no trouble finding a place. July 15 to August 15 and summer weekends are most crowded. I stayed at the Pickwick Hotel, 93 Albert Road, Blackpool FY1 4PW, tel. (0253)24229, £9/person. It was clean, friendly and cheery enough but nothing special.

Itinerary Options
I skip Chester on this itinerary—it's a second rate York. But, many people love old Chester, and we drive right by it today. If you leave Ruthin at 9:00 you could have a good two-hour look at Chester. Also, if you'd like an especially big dose of Coney Island you could go right to Blackpool.

DAY 13
THE WINDERMERE LAKE DISTRICT

Blackpool to the Cumbrian Lake District is another great contrast. After a short two-hour drive we'll be in the heart of Wordsworth Country. If you never were a poet, here's your chance in a land where nature rules and man keeps a wide-eyed but low profile. Today we'll get oriented in the Lake District, enjoying a boat ride and the best six-mile walk it has to offer, before getting set up in the most remote and scenic accommodations of the trip.

Suggested Schedule

9:00 am	Breakfast (earlier if possible—unlikely in Blackpool).
9:30 am	Drive north.
11:00 am	Brockhole National Park Visitors Center. Orientation movie, then get map and guide, talk to info man, browse through exhibits, picnic on grounds or lunch in cafeteria.
1:00 pm	Drive to Ullswater, park at Glenridding.
1:45 pm	Buy boat ticket.
2:00 pm	Catch boat.
2:35 pm	Hike from Howtown to Glenridding.
5:30 pm	Drive to B&B.

Transportation

Follow the M55 and M6 Motorways north from Blackpool past Lancaster, exiting on the A591 through Kendal and the town of Windermere to the Brockhole National Park Centre, half-way between Windermere and Ambleside on A591. From Brockhole take the tiny road northeast directly to Troutbeck and then follow A592 to the town of Glenridding and lovely Ullswater. Just before Glenridding, turn right to the car park and boat dock (40p self-service parking stickers). We'll catch the 2:00 boat, sail for 35 minutes and walk 3 hours back to the car. Now we drive north along the lake, turning left on A5091 and then left again on A66 to Keswick and to your B&B over Newlands.

Sightseeing Highlights
▲▲**Brockhole National Park Visitors Centre**—This is the place to start your visit to the Lake District. Fine intro slide shows daily at 11:00 and 2:30, info desk, organized walks, special exhibits, book shop, cafeteria, gardens, nature walks, large car park. In a big old stately house on the shores of Windermere between Ambleside and the town of Windermere on A591. Open daily 10:00-6:00, £1 entrance fee, tel. (09662)2231. Our important goal is to arrive here from Blackpool by 11:00 to catch the orientation show. Use the bookshop to buy the Ordnance Survey "Lake District Tourist Map" (£2.40) and a guidebook. I enjoyed the refreshingly opinionated *Good Guide to the Lakes* by Hunter Davies

(£2.95). Go over your plans (Ullswater ferry schedule) with the info person.

The whole district is dotted with Tourist Information Centers. All are helpful, especially for their specific locality. Use them. Ask for advice.

▲▲▲**Ullswater hike and boat ride**—Ullswater is considered the most beautiful lake in the area, and this hike is a great way to enjoy it. Park your car at the Glenridding dock on the south end of the lake. Be sure to catch the 2:00 boat (It's best to to get there 20 minutes early in summer; 35-minute ride; £1.30; tel. Glenridding 229 for info) to the first stop, Howtown, halfway up the lake. Then spend three hours hiking and dawdling along the well marked path by the lake south to Patterdale and then along the road back to your car in Glenridding. Good views, varied terrain, a few bridges and farms along the way. I did the walk in tennis shoes in 2½ hours. Bring raingear.

Cumbrian Lake District

Accommodations

The Lake District abounds with very attractive B&Bs, guest houses and youth hostels. It needs all of them when summer hordes threaten the serenity of this Romantics' mecca. The region is most crowded on Sundays and from July 20 to September 1st. Saturdays are not bad. With a car to shop around in, you should have no trouble finding a room, but for a particular place it's best to call ahead.

Birkrigg Farm—This is the perfect farmhouse B&B for this trip. Mrs. Margaret Beatty serves visitors with a comfy lounge, evening tea (good for socializing with her other guests), classy breakfast, territorial view, perfect peace and a hot water bottle to warm up your bed (farmhouses lack central heating). She's open late March through early November, charges £7.50 and does a fine £4 dinner for guests who order in advance (a good idea). Her 220-acre farm is shown on the Ordnance Survey map, on the tiny road halfway between Braithwaite (near Keswick) and Buttermere. Birkrigg Farm, Newlands, Keswick, Cumbria, CA125TS, tel. (0596)82278.

For Village B&B's try the beautiful Valley of Borrowdale (south off Derwent Water). The village of Grange is nice but Rosthwaite is better. **The Yew Tree Farm** (Hazel Ralph, tel. (059684)675) and **The Nook Farm** (Carole Jackson, tel. (059684)677) each charge £4 and are very old—I mean their houses: saggy floors, thick whitewashed walls, small doorways and hearthocentric (no central heating). If you're interested in farm noises and the old world, these are for you.

Youth Hostels—The Lake District has 30 youth hostels and needs more. Most are great old buildings, handy sources of info, and fun socially. In the summer you'll need to call ahead. For our plan consider the **King George VI Memorial Hostel**—good food, royal setting, ¼ mile south of Buttermere Village on Honister Pass Road, tel. (059685)254. Also, the **Lougthwaite Hostel**, secluded in Borrowdale Valley just south of Rosthwaite—well run, drying rooms, tel. (059684)257. Remember, hostels are marked on most good maps with a red triangle.

Itinerary Options

Consider seeing Wordsworth's Dove Cottage today rather than tomorrow. Skip the hike, do the Info Center and Wordsworth's Dove Cottage. Or, skip breakfast and do Brockhole Center 10:00-11:30, Dove Cottage 12:00-1:00, and then the hike. Or, skip the Info Center and do Dove Cottage. Any of these options make tomorrow much easier by doing Wordsworth's place today.

DAY 14
THE WINDERMERE LAKE DISTRICT

We'll enjoy an easy day today, with a little joy-riding, choosing from a
couple of great Lake District hikes, and visiting the humble house of
William Wordsworth, the poet whose appreciation of nature and back-
to-basics lifestyle put this area on the map. If you need a vacation from
your vacation, use this day to just vegetate and recharge.

Suggested Schedule	
9:00 am	Slow breakfast, enjoy your farm.
10:00 am	Explore Buttermere, Honister Pass, Borrowdale.
12:00	Lunch and drive to Grasmere.
1:00 pm	Tour Wordsworth's Dove Cottage and museum.
3:00 pm	Drive to Keswick, see town and catch circular boat (clockwise) to High Brandlehow Pier. Walk along lake to Hawsend Pier. Catch boat to Keswick.
6:00 pm	Drive home (visiting Castlerigg Stone Circle if you have time and energy).

Transportation
Nothing is very far from Keswick and Derwent Water. The entire region
is just 30 miles by 30 miles. By all means get a good map, get off the big
roads and leave the car at least occasionally for some walking. In the
summer, the Keswick-Ambleside-Windermere-Bowness area suffers
from congestion. Larger lakes are served by old "steamers," and any T.I.
can give you local schedules.

Sightseeing Highlights
▲▲▲**Dove Cottage**—Wordsworth spent his most productive years
(1799-1813) in this well-preserved old cottage on the edge of Grasmere.
Today it is the obligatory sight for any visit to the area. Even if you're
not a fan (and I'm not), Wordsworth's style of "plain living and high
thinking," his appreciation of nature and his basic Romanticism are very
appealing. The cottage tour is excellent as is the adjoining museum.
Even a speedy and jaded museum-goer will want at least an hour here.
Open 9:30-5:30, April-September (Sundays from 11:00) and 10:00-4:30
off-season. £2.
Rydal Mount—Wordsworth's final, more high-class home, lovely
garden and view. It lacks the charm of Dove Cottage, and is worthwhile
only for Wordsworth fans.
▲▲**Derwent Water**—One of the region's most beautiful and most
popular lakes. With five islands, a good circular boat service, plenty of
trails and the pleasant town of Keswick at its north end, the lake enter-
tains. The roadside views aren't much, so walk or cruise. I'd suggest a
combo hike/sail trip around the lake and an hour in Keswick (good
shops and tourist info). The boats go every 15 minutes in each direction
and make seven stops on each 50-minute roundtrip. The best walk is

between High Brandlehow and Hawesend. (There's a large car park at the Keswick pier and a small one above Hawesend.)

High Ridge Hike—The best "king of the mountain" feeling. Park your car at Hawesend, hike up along the ridge to Cat Bells, past the peak to Black Crag and down to High Brandlehow. From there take the easy path along the shore of Derwent Water back to your Hawesend starting point.

▲▲▲**A Waterfall and Two Tarns**—For a rewarding 2 or 3 hour hike park your car south of Borrowdale at the end of a long dead-end road to Seathwaite. Go through the farm, cross the river, continue along the river (it's difficult to follow the trail but keep along the river) and up a steep rocky climb to the Taylor Gill Force—a 140 foot waterfall. There's a hundred yards of rocky scramble here but the trail gets good at the falls. Keep walking to two lovely remote "tarns" (bodies of water too small to be a lake), circling the Seathwaite Fell to Stockley Bridge and following the bridle path back to your car. For an easy version, just hike to the first tarn and backtrack, eventually taking a right turn leading to Stockley Bridge (get advice at Keswick T.I.).

▲▲**Buttermere**—This is the ideal little lake with a lovely mile stroll around it offering nonstop lakeland beauty. If you're not a hiker but kind of wish you were, take this walk. If you're very short on time, at least stop here for a short break. A great road over the rugged Honister Pass connects Buttermere with Borrowdale and Derwent Water.

▲**Castlerigg Stone Circle**—38 stones, 90 feet across, 3,000 years old, mysteriously laid out on a line between the two tallest peaks on the horizon. Great setting. Just south of the A66, east of Keswick, well signposted from A66. Look for "stone circle" exit.

DAY 15
LAKE DISTRICT
TO WEST COAST OF SCOTLAND

Today we drive for six hours to Oban, the gateway to the Hebrides,
Scotland's wild and windblown western islands. The last half of the
journey is scenic, taking us from big and burly Glasgow along the famous Loch Lomond, deep into the powerful mountains, forests, valleys
and lochs of Scotland's west country and to the edge of the Highlands.

Suggested Schedule

9:00 am	Leave Lake District (stopping at the Castlerigg Stone Circle if you haven't yet). Drive 3 hours to Glasgow.
1:00 pm	Stop along Loch Lomond for picnic lunch. Drive on, 3 hours from Glasgow to Oban, enjoying the rugged scenery enroute.
4:00 pm	Arrive in Oban, go first to tourist office and then to your B&B.

Transportation
From Keswick take A66 to M6 and speed non-stop north. You'll cross
Hadrian's Wall and into Scotland, where the Motorway ends but the
road (A74) stays great all the way to Glasgow. A74 will become M74.
Follow it to M8, which dissolves right into the big city. The signs are
there but tricky. Follow signs for A82, Dumbarton until you're out of
Glasgow. After Dumbarton, it's A82 to Loch Lomond. The lakeside road
is lovely but often congested. Keep heading north through Crianlarich,
taking A85 west through more beauty into Oban.

Sightseeing Highlights
This "gateway to the isles" has ferries coming and going all day long.
The **Isle of Mull** (3rd largest in Scotland, most scenic, 300 miles of
coastline, castle, 3,169-foot-high mountain) is worth a day. Just beyond
it, the historic island of **Iona**, (St. Columba brought Christianity here in
590 AD, abbey and thousands of visitors), can be visited easily as part of
a tour from Oban. A tour beats taking your car on the ferry (too expensive). Get specifics from the excellent T.I. (Open Monday-Friday, 9:00-
9:00, Saturday, 9:00-6:00, Sunday, 3:00-6:00, tel. 63123).
   The stark but very green **Island of Kerrera**, just opposite Oban (6
boats a day, 75p, from Gallanach, 2 miles south of Oban), is a quick and
easy opportunity to get that romantic island experience. Enjoy a walk,
solitude and the sea. The islands of Seil and Luing, a short drive south,
are another good sidetrip.
   Oban itself has plenty going on in the summer. The T.I. has handouts
listing everything from saunas to laundromats to horse riding and what
to do in the rain. Use them.

Accommodations

Oban has plenty of B&B's for its many visitors. The Tourist Info will fill you with specifics and can find you a room if my suggestions don't work.

Strathlachlan Guest House. This is a winner. Mrs. Rena Anderson charges £8 for a place that's quiet, clean, stocking-feet cozy, crackerjack friendly and chocolate-box tidy. There's a great lounge, easy parking, good central location 2 blocks off the water just past Jay's Tearoom. 2 Strathaven Terrace, Oban, Argyll, tel. 0631/63861.

Achanmara Hotel—On the "Esplanade" waterfront promenade. A lovely location with an island view, 3 minutes from downtown. This is a grand old hotel with hotel-style formality, but charging a reasonable £10. tel. 62683

Rahoy Lodge—On Gallanach Road about a mile south of town, overlooking the beach and islands. A bit eccentric—a "lived in" lodge. £8.50. tel. (0631)62301

Youth Hostel, on the "Esplanade," alongside the finest hotels in town, in a grand building with a grand piano, and a harbor/island view. £3, tel. 62025. Open only April-October.

Food

Oban has plenty of eating options. In season, try to mix dinner and some Scottish folk entertainment. **McTavish's Kitchen** on the central George Street is a plain looking cafeteria which serves hearty cheap food and live folk music and dance on most nights. **Jay's Tearoom** nearby is a comfy place with an interesting menu for a light meal.

DAY 16
HIGHLANDS, LOCH NESS, SCENIC DRIVE

Today is mostly driving—but joy-riding—with a chance to see the harsh Highland beauty of Glencoe, the engineering beauty of the Caladonian Canal, and the soft beauty of Loch Ness—which is worth a look even if you don't see the monster. How far you get today depends on the weather, the traffic and your eagerness to get to bonnie Edinburgh.

Suggested Schedule	
9:00 am	Leave Oban.
10:00 am	Explore Glencoe.
11:00 am	Drive Glencoe to Fort Augustus.
12:00	Loch Ness Castle, picnic, Monster business.
3:00 pm	Culloden Battlefield.
4:00 pm	Drive south.
7:00 pm	Possibly set up in Edinburgh.

Transportation
Scotland's roads have improved remarkably in the last few years. You'll make great time on good, mostly two-lane roads today unless traffic gets in the way. Americans are generally very timid about passing. Study the British. If you don't pass, diesel and large trucks may be your memory of "Day 16."
From Oban, follow the coastal A828 noticing the enchanting ruined island castle on your left a few minutes north of town. At Loch Leven go in to Glencoe. Skip the town and drive 10 miles inland until you hit the vast, depressingly flat Rannoch Moor. Then make a U-turn and return through the valley. Continue north, over the bridge, past boring Fort William and on towards Loch Ness. For 60 miles you'll follow the Caladonian Canal and A82 to Inverness. Follow signs to A9 (south to Perth) and just as you leave Inverness (not worth a stop) turn east off A9 onto B9006 to the Culloden Battlefield Visitors Center. Back on A9 it's a wonderfully speedy and very scenic road (A9, M90, A90) all the way to Edinburgh. If traffic is light, you can drive from Inverness to Edinburgh in 2½ hours.

Sightseeing Highlights
▲▲Glencoe—This is the essence of the wild, powerful, and stark beauty of the Highlands (and I think excuses the hurried tourist from needing to go north of Inverness). Along with its scenery, Glencoe offers a good dose of bloody clan history. Stop in at the visitors center to learn about the "murder under trust" of 1692, when the Campbells massacred the sleeping MacDonalds and the valley got its nickname, "The Weeping Glen."

Ben Nevis—At Fort William you'll pass Ben Nevis, Britain's highest peak (over 4400 feet). Thousands of visitors walk to its summit each year but we'll just hope for a clear day and admire her from the car.

▲**Caladonian Canal**—Scotland is sliced in half by three lochs (Oich, Lochy, and Ness) connected in the early 1800s with a series of canals and locks by the great engineer, Telford. As you drive the 60 miles from Ft. William to Inverness follow Telford's work—40 miles of lakes, 20 miles of canals, locks, raising ships from sea level to 51 feet (Ness) to 93 feet (Lochy) to 106 feet (Oich). Fort Augustus is the best stop. Drop into its free museum for more information.

▲**Loch Ness**—I'll admit, I had my eyes on the water. The local tourist industry thrives on the legend of the Loch Ness monster. It's a thrilling thought, and there have been several seemingly reliable "sightings" (priests, policemen, and now sonar images) but I didn't buy it. The Loch Ness Monster Info Center (open 9:00 am—9:30 pm daily, £1.65, in Drumnadrochit) is tacky and a disappointment; if you've got half an hour and a couple bucks to blow, see if I'm right. The nearby Urquhart Castle ruins (Monday-Friday, 9:30-7:00, Sunday and Saturday, 2:00-7:00, £1) are gloriously situated with a view of virtually the entire Loch Ness and make for a better stop than the monster center. Drumnadrochit has its Highland Games on the last Saturday of each August.

▲**Culloden Battlefield**—Bonnie Prince Charlie was defeated here in 1746. This last battle fought on British soil spelled the end of the Jacobite resistance and the fall of the clans. The visitors center makes the short detour worthwhile with a great AV show, a furnished old cottage, the memorial and other exhibits. (Daily 9:30-8:00)

Findhorn Foundation—This international spiritual community, famous for its sensitivity to nature and its tremendously green thumb greets visitors with daily 2:00 tours. 20 miles east of Inverness.

Scottish Words
ben—mountain
carn, cairn—heap of stones
creag, crag—rock, cliff
inch, innis—island
kyle—strait, firth
loch—lake
haggis—rich meat dish (bladder stuffed with sheep's pluck).
tattie—potato

Accommodations
Here's where things get murky. You can get to Edinburgh if you really push. You'll arrive late, so be sure to have a firm hold on a bed and call at 5:00 with your ETA (See Edinburgh Accommodations below).

A more relaxed plan is to find a room somewhere between Culloden and Pitlochry. Inverness has plenty of rooms—but not much reason to stop. I'd head south to find a place in one of many pleasant towns along the A9. Pitlochry is lovely.

DAY 17
EDINBURGH

Edinburgh is Scotland's showpiece—historical, monumental, entertaining, well-organized—it's a tourist's delight and I think one of Europe's greatest cities. We'll have nearly two days here—and we'll need every minute.

Suggested Schedule

9:00 am	Drive into Edinburgh from the Highlands.
12:00	Arrive in Edinburgh, park in central train station lot, do your tourist information chores, have lunch in the Waverly Center downstairs, or picnic in the Princes Street Gardens. Call B&B to say you're in town. Browse through Waverly Center and the Princes Gardens.
2:00 pm	Climb Scott Monument for orientation view. Understand town lay-out: Royal Mile on ridge from castle to palace, former Nor Loch lake bed, New Georgian town.
2:30 pm	Georgian walk—down Rose Street, up Castle Street, left down George Street to Charlotte Square. Tour the Georgian House at #7. Don't miss its video.
5:00 pm	Return to car, drive to B&B, check in.

Option: if you arrived the night before, it would be best to visit the tourist office that night or first thing in the morning, and switch days 17 and 18, doing the castle and Royal Mile first, and the Georgian town with free time on the second day in Edinburgh.

Transportation
You'll be arriving the evening of Day 16 or about noon on Day 17, depending on which you favor—the country thrills of the Highlands or the city thrills of Edinburgh. Either way, follow the signs to city center and the center's intersection of Princes Street and Waverly Bridge.

Arriving in the evening—Park wherever you can and run into the tourist info office (open till 9:00 in July and August) before driving to your B&B.

Mid-day—Turn on to Waverly Bridge, then left into the train station, park in the huge central parking lot and climb past the Waverly Shopping Center to the Tourist Info. That evening, drive to your B&B. (Call your B&B upon arrival to explain your plans.)

You won't need your car again until you leave Edinburgh. City buses (routes listed in basic 20p city map at T.I.; average fare 20 to 30p) and taxis (easy to flag down, several handy pick up points, 70p drop charge, average ride, downtown to the B&B district—£1.50) are easy and inexpensive while parking and traffic are a real headache. Within town nearly all sights are within walking distance.

Orientation

Edinburgh is two basic towns divided by what was once a lake. The lake (Nor Loch) was drained and is now a lovely park and community center containing the helpful tourist information center, Waverly Shopping Center, the train station and parking lot, the starting point for most city bus tours, the festival office, and National Gallery.

The old town was actually a volcanic ridge running south of the lake. This became packed with historic and fascinating buildings bounded on the summit by the great castle and on the bottom by the Holyrood Palace. This is the "Royal Mile" which, in its day, was called the most crowded city in the world. Houses, shops and arcades were narrow and tall with "closes," or little courtyards, connected to "High Street" by narrow lanes or even tunnels. This colorful jumble is the tourist's Edinburgh.

To alleviate crowding, the lake was drained and a magnificent Georgian city, today's "New Town," was laid out to the north. Georgian Edinburgh, like Bath, shined with broad boulevards, straight streets, square squares, circular circuses, and elegant mansions decked out in colonnades, pediments, and sphinxes all in the proud style of 200 years ago.

Edinburgh Centre

1 - TRAIN STATION, CENTRAL CAR PARK
2 - TOURIST INFO, WAVERLY CENTER
3 - CASTLE ESPLANADE, TOP OF ROYAL MILE
4 - GLADSTONE'S LAND, LADY STAIR'S HOUSE MUSEUM
5 - ST. GILE'S CATHEDRAL
6 - WALTER SCOTT MONUMENT
7 - JOHN KNOX HOUSE, MUSEUM OF CHILDHOOD
8 - HUNTLY HOUSE, CRAFTCENTER
9 - GEORGIAN HOUSE, NO. 7 CHARLOTTE STREET
10 - WAVERLY BRIDGE
11 - NATIONAL GALLERY
12 - CALDONIAN HOTEL
13 - 1 MILE SOUTH OF MAP: ROYAL COMMONWEALTH POOL, BEST B+Bs ON DALKEITH RD. (WHICH BECOMES A68 SOUTH TO ENGLAND)

Sightseeing Highlights

Be organized with this list of sights to get the most out of your two days in Edinburgh. Your first stop on arrival must be the Tourist Information Center in its new location, central as can be atop the Waverly Center on Princes Street. Open 8:30-9:00 in July and August, 8:30-8:00 in June and September, and 9:00-6:00 off season, Sundays only from 11:00. Tel. (031)557-2727.

Buy a city map (20p) and city "Official Guide Book" (£1.50) and "Edinburgh, a Guide to the Royal City" (85p), and pick up "What's On" and "Walking Tours in the City Center" brochures. Confirm your sight-seeing plans and hours as described below, and ask about walking tours down the Royal Mile, evening events and entertainment, and mid-day concerts in the park.

▲**Walter Scott Monument**—An elaborate neo-Gothic building (like Albert Memorial and Houses of Parliament in London) honoring the great author, one of Edinburgh's many illustrious sons. (Built 1844, 200 feet high, 287 steps to a fine city orientation view.)

▲**Rose Street**—The New (or Georgian) Town's most interesting street. Pedestrians only, cute shops, and 21 pubs. A pleasant stroll by day and quite a crawl after dark.

▲▲**Georgian Edinburgh**—The grand George Street connects St. Andrew and Charlotte Squares. This is the centerpiece of the elegantly planned New Town. Don't miss the refurbished Georgian House at #7 Charlotte Square with an interesting video introduction and a lady in each lavish room bursting with stories and trivia. Open Monday-Saturday, 10:00-5:00, Sunday 2:00-5:00.

Accommodations

Edinburgh, the festival city, is packed in the summer. But it has lots of B&B's, hotels and hostels with a super tourist office to make the needed connections.

The annual festival fills the city every year from the beginning of August until about September 8. In 1986, July will be even worse, when Edinburgh hosts The Commonwealth Games. Conventions, school holidays and other surprises can make room-finding tough at almost any time. Call ahead, use the Tourist Office or at least arrive early.

The best B&B district is, without a doubt, south of town. You'll find street after street of B&Bs south of the Royal Commonwealth Pool between Orange Road and Dalkeith Road. This area is a twenty-minute walk from the Royal Mile, well served by city buses, comfortably safe and loaded with eateries, laundromats, shops, etc.

Millfield Guest House—Mrs. Liz Broomfield's place is great with an entertaining proprietor, quiet street, and easy parking, around the corner town, the bus stop; comfy TV lounge, good phone for long distance calls. £9, tel. (031)667-4428, at 12 Marchhall Road (just east off Dalkeith Road, south of pool).

Kilmaurs Guest House—Just down the street from the Millfield Guest House, Mr. and Mrs. Ross make you feel right at home—clean, TV in room, Mr. Ross loosening things up with typical husband-of-the-B&B-lady's terrible jokes, £10, at 9 Kilmaur Road, tel. (031)667-8315.

Ravensneuk Guest House is nearby at 11 Blacket Ave, tel. (031)667-5347, across Dalkeith Road. At 10£, it's a good third choice.

These three B&B's (and many more nearby) are well served by buses. On Dalkeith, #14, 21, 36 and 49 (all but #2) take you downtown. On Minto St. #3, 7, 8, 18, 31 & 37 do the same. The handy laundromat on 208 Dalkeith is open Monday-Friday 8:30-5:00, Saturday and Sunday 10:00-2:00, charges £2.30 for a self-serve load. Pay just 40p more, they'll do it for you. Wonderful take-out Chinese food on Minto Street, and handy cafeteria overlooking huge Commonwealth Pool.

Youth Hostels—The T.I. has a list of cheap beds. The best hostel in town is the **Bruntsfield YA**, on a park, at #7 Bruntsfield Crescent. Well-run, £3, buses #11, 15, 16 to and from Princes Street, tel. 447-2994. The other hostel is also good (337-1120). The YWCAs at 226-3842, 225-3608 and 229-4850 are for women only, open all year.

Food

Restaurants are good, plentiful, and rather expensive. For cheap eating, go ethnic—especially Chinese take out and pub lunches (Scottish pubs don't serve evening meals). Or try the **Commonwealth Pool** cafeteria, or the **Waverly Center Food Circus**, a ring of flashy trendy fast food joints offering a plastic galaxy of choices. At Waverly try **McTavishes** for hearty, inexpensive, traditional Scottish specialties like haggis. Or picnic. The T.I. has brochures and books on dining locally.

DAY 18
EDINBURGH

Today, we'll continue our look at Edinburgh, visiting the castle, exploring our way down the history-packed Royal Mile to the Holyrood Palace. Our Scottish finale will be an evening of folk fun, food and music.

Suggested Schedule

9:00 am	Breakfast and bus to High Street or taxi to Castle Esplanade.
9:30 am	Tour castle.
11:00 am	Do Royal Mile: Gladstone Land, Lady Stair's House, Pub lunch, St. Giles Church, Knox's House, Huntly House, Craft Center.
4:00 pm	Tour Holyrood Palace.
7:00 pm	Scottish Evening—dinner show in hotel or simple dinner and folk music in a pub.

Sightseeing Highlights

▲▲▲**Royal Mile**—One of Europe's most interesting historic walks, whether you follow a local guide (daily, free, during the summer) or do-it-yourself with a Royal Mile guidebook. Each step of the way is entertaining. Start at the top and loiter your way down hill to the palace. Below are the top sights of the Royal Mile—working downhill.

▲▲**The Edinburgh Castle**—The fortified birthplace of the city 1,300 years ago, this is the imposing symbol of Edinburgh. Start with the free 20-minute guided intro tour, leaving every few minutes from inside the gate. Don't miss the Scottish National War Memorial, Banqueting Hall with fine Scottish Crown Jewels, the room full of Battle of Culloden mementos, St. Margaret's Chapel (oldest building in town), the giant cannon and the city view from the ramparts (best seen in that order). Allow 90 minutes including the tour. Open 9:30-5:30, Monday-Saturday, Sunday 11:00-5:50. Costs £2.

▲▲**Gladstone's Land**—Your best look at a typical 16th—17th century house with lived-in furnished interior and guides in each room. The best Royal Mile photo is from the top floor window. Open Monday-Saturday 10:00-5:00, Sunday 2:00-5:00.

▲**Lady Stair's House**—An interesting house from 1622 filled with manuscripts and knick-knacks of Scotland's three greatest literary figures, Robert Burns, Sir Walter Scott and Robert Louis Stevenson. Interesting for anyone, fantastic for fans. Open 10:00-6:00, Closed Sundays.

St. Giles Cathedral—Interesting Gothic church, don't miss the ornate, medieval thistle chapel or the Scottish crown steeple.

John Knox's House—Fascinating if you're into Reformation history. This fine 16th century house is filled with things from the life of the Great Reformer. Monday-Saturday, 10:00-5:00, closed on Sundays.

Huntly House—Another old house full of old stuff. It's free and worth a look for its early Edinburgh history. Don't miss the copy of the National Covenant written on an animal skin, and the sketches of pre-Georgian Edinburgh with its lake still wet. Open 10:00-6:00, closed Sundays.

Crafts center in the Acheson House (in courtyard next to Huntly House)—Full of entertaining network by 300 local crafts people. Free.

▲**Holyrood Palace**—This bottom end of the Royal Mile is the queen's residence when she's in town. Guided tours only of the royal apartments, state apartment, and lots of rich furnishings, paintings and history. Open Monday-Saturday 9:30-6:00, Sunday 10:30-5:15 (Closed when in use).

▲**Arthur's Seat**—The 823-foot volcanic mountain surrounded by a fine park overlooking Edinburgh. A 30-minute hike up from the Holyrood Palace or from the Commonwealth Pool, with a rewarding view. The easiest "I climbed a mountain" feeling I've ever had.

Princes Street Gardens—This grassy former lake bed separates Edinburgh's new and old towns with a wonderful escape from the citiness of it all. Plenty of free concerts and dancing in the summer and the oldest floral clock in the world. Join local office workers in a picnic lunch break.

National Gallery—An elegant neo-Classical building with a small but impressive collection of European masterpieces and the best look you'll get at Scottish paintings. Monday-Saturday 10:00-5:00, Sunday 2:00-5:00.

Royal Commonwealth Games Swimming Pool—The biggest pool I've ever seen. Open to the public, swim-suit and towel rentals, good cafeteria, weights, saunas, etc.

City bus tours—Edinburgh offers a stunning array of tours taking you around the city or around Scotland. The half-day tours of greater Edinburgh take over where your feet leave off. One-day tours can take you as far as the Western Islands, Oban, and Loch Ness. Tours leave from the Mound, near the train station.

Greyhound Races—If you've never seen dog racing, this is a fun night out offering great people-watching, and a chance to lose some money gambling. About two nights a week at Powderhall Stadium (see "What's On" schedule).

Edinburgh Crystal—Blowing, molding, cutting, polishing, engraving, The Edinburgh Crystal Company gives by far the best glass works tour I've seen (puts Venice to shame). 10 miles south of town (A701) in Penicuik. 45-minute tour leave regularly from 9:00-3:30 (75p, except free from 9:00-10:00). There's a shop full of "bargain" second quality pieces, video show, good cafeteria. (Consider half-day tours from the Mound or doing it on your way south. Call first, (0968)75128, and try to avoid the 11:15-12:45 factory lunch break.

Stirling Castle—Skip it. It's very famous, but is currently used as a barracks—a disappointment. The town is pleasantly medieval, however, and many commute (one hour by train) to the more hectic Edinburgh from there.

▲▲▲**The Edinburgh Festival**—August and September—One of *the* events of Europe, the annual festival turns Edinburgh into a carnival of culture. There's enough music, dance, art and drama to make even the most jaded tourist drool with excitement. Every day is jammed with formal and spontaneous fun.

The festival rages from mid-August through September's first week with the "fringe festival" and the Military Tatoo starting a few days early. Many city sights run on extended hours and those that normally close on Sundays don't. Local students give free Royal Mile walking tours, and all in all it's a glorious time to be in Edinburgh.

Major events sell out well in advance, but every day is packed with top-notch "ticket at the door" opportunities. Look into tickets from London at the start of your tour and do whatever you can to get a ticket to the massed bands, drums, bagpipes and sometimes even elephants of the Military Tattoo (nightly except Thursday and Sunday, at the castle, tel. 225-1188 for info). Keep in mind that the equally wonderful and more informal Fringe Festival (tel. 226-5257) has literally hundreds of events that only sell tickets at the door. Your major festival worry is getting a room. After that get a program—and you're a hyper kid in a cultural wading pool. If you do manage to hit the festival, be sure to add at least a third day here.

Shopping—The best shopping is along Princes Street (don't miss elegant old Jenner's Department Store), the mod and flashy Waverly Center, Rose Street and the Royal Mile. Hours—9:00-5:30, staying open late on Thursdays.

▲▲**Folk Music**—Edinburgh offers either folk music in pubs or more organized "Scottish folk evenings," generally in more expensive hotels. For from £10 to £20 at several hotels on nearly any night you can enjoy a traditional—or at least what the tourists believe is traditional—meal with the full slate of swirling kilts, blaring bagpipes and colorful Scottish folk dancing. Plenty of specifics at T.I. or in "What's On."

For a basic informal evening of folk music, find the right pub. My favorite Scottish band, the "North Sea Gas," plays every Friday, 8:30-11:00, free at Platform One in the Caledonian Hotel on Princes Street. Pubs that feature folk music almost nightly are the White Hart (Grassmarket), Fables (West Port), Royal Oak (Infirmary St.) and the Waverly Bar (St. Mary St.). "What's On" lists current folk music spots, and nearly any cabbie knows a hot spot or can find one by asking on his radio. (In general, cabbies are a great ace-in-the-hole source of information.)

DAY 19
EDINBURGH—HADRIAN'S WALL—DURHAM

From Edinburgh we head south, filling today with fascinating sights
from the years 100, 1200, and 1900 AD. We'll visit Hadrian's Wall, ancient Rome's northernmost boundary, marvel at Durham Cathedral, England's greatest Norman building, and relive the dawn of our century at
the great Beamish Folk Museum.

Suggested Schedule

8:30 am	Leave Edinburgh.
11:00 am	Arrive at Hadrian's Wall, tour fort, museum, take a walk along wall, lunch.
1:00 pm	Drive to Beamish Museum.
2:00 pm	Beamish Open Air Museum.
5:00 pm	Drive to Durham.
5:30 pm	Arrive Durham, visit T.I., get B&B, tour cathedral.

Transportation

From Edinburgh, Dalkeith Road leads south, becoming A68. (There's a
handy supermarket on the left just as you leave Dalkeith Town, ten minutes south of Edinburgh, parking behind). A68 takes you all the way to
Hadrian's Wall in 2½ hours. You'll pass Jedburgh and its abbey after one
hour. (There's a tour bus delight just before Jedburgh with kilt makers,
woolens, and a sheep skin shop. In Jedburgh, across from a lovely
abbey, is a good visitors center and public toilets.) The England/Scot-
land border (great view and "Mr. Softy" ice cream and tea caravan) is a
fun quick stop. Before Hexham, roller-coaster down A6079 two miles to
B6318. This great little road follows the Roman Wall westward. Notice
the Wall on its trenches on either side as you go. After ten minutes and
several "severe dips" (if there's a certified nerd or bozo in the car, these
road signs add a lot to a photo portrait) pull into the Housestead's
Roman Fort information center. The Roman fort is on the right.

After your visit, take the small road past Vindolanda (another Roman
fort and museum) to the A69. Go east past Hexham, then south on the
A68. After a few miles turn east on B6278 through lovely little Snods
Edge, through Blackhill to Stanley. The Beamish Museum is well signposted between Stanley and Chester-le-Street.

After the museum follow the signs west past Chester to the Motorway.
Head south. Just before you enter Durham's old town center (Cathedral
and castle) turn left into the modern high-rise parking lot. (Parking in
old Durham is miserable). From the 7th floor a walkway takes you right
into the old town.

The route from Durham south to the North York Moors is tricky.
Whatever you do, don't get sucked into the Stockton-Middlesbrough
mess. Take the Motorway all the way to Darlington before heading east
along A67.

Sightseeing Highlights

▲▲▲**Hadrian's Wall**—One of England's most thought-provoking sights. The Romans built this great stone wall during the reign of the Emperor Hadrian (around 130 AD) to protect England from invading Scottish tribes. It stretches 74 miles from coast to coast. Defended by nearly 20,000 troops with castles every mile, it was flanked by ditches, 15 feet high and wide enough to allow chariots to race from mile castle to mile castle. Today several chunks of the wall, ruined forts and museums attract visitors.

By far the best single stop is the Housesteads Fort with a fine museum, national park info center (with car park and snack bar), and the best preserved segment of the wall surrounded by powerful scenery (open daily 10:00-6:00). From Housesteads, hike west along the Wall. Vindolanda, a larger Roman fort and museum, is just south of the wall and worth a visit only if you devoured the Housesteads museum and are still hungry.

▲▲▲**Beamish Open Air Museum**—A huge and unique center that energetically takes its visitors back to turn-of-the-century Northumbria. You'll need three hours to explore the 1900 town, train station, mining camp and working farm. This isn't wax, it's real. Attendants at each stop explain everything, a video show orients you and an old tramway saves the wear and tear on your feet. Open 10:00-6:00 daily, well worth £2.50. This is the only museum I've seen covering the dawn of our century.

▲▲**Durham Cathedral**—This is the best —and least altered—Norman Cathedral in England . . . and the only one in this itinerary. Study the difference between this heavy Romanesque fortress of worship and the light-filled Gothic of later centuries. Pick up the 10p guide, climb the 300 steps and pay the 50 pence for a great view from the tower. There's also a good cafeteria. Open 7:15-8:00 pm daily, until 5:00 pm September-May, 5:15 evensong services.

The old town of Durham cuddles the cathedral, surrounded on 3 sides by its river. It has a medieval cobbled atmosphere and a cute market just off the main square, but still is exciting only for its cathedral.

Accommodations—It's your option:

Durham—This is the easiest plan, stopping early and not having to rush Day 19. You'll be cutting the North York Moors short to spend the evening in the pleasant medieval city of Durham. Call ahead or visit the tourist info upon arrival, before visiting the cathedral. (T.I. open Monday-Friday 9:00-6:00, Saturday 9:00-5:00, Sunday 2:00-5:00, tel. 43720, leaves list of vacancies on door after hours.)

The Durham Castle is a student residence renting out its 100 singles and 30 doubles from mid-July through late September (B&B £10, tel (0385)65481). B&B district is west of center (telephone numbers 64621, 68852, 68070, 42966, 64064, 41020-all B&B's on the Avenue or Crossgate).

For dinner the **House of Andrews** (at #73 Saddler St. in the old town) and the **Traveler's Rest** pub (on Clay Path Street behind the T.I.) are both good.

Staithes—Captain Cook's boyhood town, a salty tumble of ancient buildings bunny-hopping down to a cramped little harbor. It's located on the coast just north of Whitby, a two hour drive from Durham. Only one guest house, right on the water, the **Harborside Guest House**, £10. Just your basic bed, in a setting you'll never forget. Call first, (0947)840577.

Whitby—A fun resort town full of Coney Island-type amusements. Lots of B&B's, a great abbey, people scene. Visiting here will rush your day, but if you want a mini-Blackpool, go for it. Like Staithes, just a short ride to the Moors.

On the north edge of the North York Moors—To get an early start in the Moors, leave Durham by 6:00 and find a place somewhere between Guisborough, Danby and Goathland. There are plenty of countryside B&Bs.

DAY 20
NORTH YORK MOORS AND YORK

Today, we'll drive through the harsh heart of the North York Moors for a good dose of its special stark beauty. Then we'll set up and orient ourselves in York, one of England's most exciting cities.

Suggested Schedule

8:30 am	Leave your Durham B&B at 8:00 (or 9:30 if you're already in Moor country).
10:00 am	Danby Lodge—North York Moors Visitors Center. Tour exhibit, pick up map, get help with Moors plan.
11:00 am	Drive over Moors, short stop at Hutton le Hole.
12:00	Drive to York.
1:00 pm	Arrive York, check into B&B, park car for good, visit Tourist Info, lunch in King's Manor.
2:15 pm	Walking tour of city (at 7:00 pm in summer).
4:30 pm	Railroad Museum or free in old town.

Sightseeing Highlights

▲**Danby Lodge**—North York Moors Visitors Center, ideal for your moors orientation. It's a grand old lodge offering exhibits, special shows and nature walks, an info desk with plenty of books and maps, brass rubbing, a cafeteria, and brochures on several good walks that start right there. Open daily 10:00-5:00.

▲**North Yorkshire Moors Railway**—If you're tired of driving (or without wheels), this 18-mile, 50-minute steam engine ride from Grosmont and Goethland to Pickering goes through some of the best parts of the moor almost hourly. For info call (0751)72508. For taped schedule info—73535. Pickering is worth a stopover—a rural life museum, castle, and a market on Mondays.

▲**Hutton le Hole**—Postcard-pretty town with the fine little Ryedale Museum, showing "farmlife in the moors"—reconstructed and furnished 18th century local buildings. Use the nearby car park and the public toilets. Open daily 11:00-6:00, April-October.

Castle Howard—Especially popular now since the filming of *Brideshead Revisited*, this is a fine palatial home, but Blenheim's better.

Rievaulx Abbey—A highlight of the North York Moors but a rerun of fine old abbeys we've already seen.

York

York is a walker's delight but a driver's purgatory. Don't even think of taking the car through the old city gates. Park near Bootham Street. All sights are within walking distance, and if you like, you can pay £1.50 for an all day pass on the yellow bus circuit that goes around and around constantly, connecting the major sights (with commentary, pick up flier at T.I.).

Sightseeing Highlights—York

Tourist Information—Your first stop. Pick up official guidebook (75p includes map) and "What's On" and confirm plans. Open Monday-Saturday, 9:00-8:00, Sunday 2:00-5:00. October-May, Monday-Saturday 9:00-5:00, closed Sunday. Tel. 21756. Walk here after parking near Bootham Street.

▲▲**Walking Tours**—Voluntary local guides give free two hour walks through York daily at 10:15 and 2:15 from April through October (plus 7:00pm in July and August). These meet next to Bootham Gate across from the T.I. in Exhibition Square. An ideal orientation.

There are many other York walking tours. The popular ghost tours go nightly and are the best of their kind in England.

▲**City Walls**—The historic walks of York provide a fine 2½ mile walk. Be sure to walk from Bootham Bar (gate) to Monk Bar for outstanding cathedral views. Open till dusk, free.

▲**Railroad Museum**—A huge national museum showing 150 fascinating years of British Railroad history. Two roundhouses of historic cars and engines including Queen Victoria's lavish royal car, the very first "stagecoaches on rails," plus video shows and much more. This is the best RR museum anywhere. Very popular, free, 10-minute walk from center, open Monday-Saturday 10:00-6:00, Sunday 2:30-6:00.

Accommodations

York has plenty of beds and, since we'll be pulling in at noon, finding a room shouldn't be too tough. The tourist office has an efficient room-finding service (tel. 21756, open 9:00-8:00). There are several student-type hostels (listed in *Let's Go* or at the T.I.). The best B&B district is just five or ten minutes from the Minster past the T.I. up Bootham Road. Try these:

York Lodge Guest House—Cozy, friendly, ideally located, and well worth £9.50—£10. Run by ten-year-old Christopher and his friendly parents, Hilary and Keith Meadley. At 64 Bootham Crescent, Bootham, York, Y037AH, tel. 0904/54289.

The Blossoms—A bigger place, very well-run but less homey, easy to find, and not so expensive, at £8. (28 Clifton Road, tel. 52391, run by Susan and Chas Bruce).

Briar Lea Guest House—Small, cozy and friendly. Ray and Judy Sutton, at 8 Longfield Terrace, tel. 0904/35061. £8.50.

Longfield House—At 2 Longfield Terrace, tel. 0904/27321, run by Mr. & Mrs. Dixon. A good value for £7.

Food

For a handy, cheap and historic lunch, try the **King's Manor**, found on Exhibition Square across from the T.I., through the courtyard on the left. (Lunch Monday-Friday 12:00-2:00). Also, **Clifton Coin-Op** on Bootham between all recommended B&Bs, open 7:30-8:00, Monday-Friday; 7:30-6:00, Saturday and Sunday.

DAY 21
YORK

On this very busy York day we'll start with a good look at its great church, wander through its wonderfully preserved medieval quarter and spend the last half of the day immersed in the past—first reliving the 1800s in the Castle Museum and then going all the way back to the town the Vikings called Jorvik.

Suggested Schedule	
9:00	Tour York Minster.
10:00	Browse through old town, Shambles.
1:00	York Castle Museum.
5:00	Jorvik Viking Center.

Sightseeing Highlights
▲▲▲**The York Minster, or Cathedral**—The pride of York, this largest Gothic church in Britain is thrilling. Pick up the "Walk Round York Minster" flier and ask at the info desk for a guided tour—available almost upon command, and very enlightening. Highlights are the fine medieval stained glass (1986 will offer a rare close-up look at the famous Rose Window in the Chatter Room), and the undercroft, showing foundations of Roman and Saxon buildings, the modern concrete save-the-church foundations, the treasure, and a moving display about the recent and tragic 1984 fire and the worldwide support for the restoration work. Open daily from 7:00. Dreary evensong daily at 5:00. Tour info at 24426.

▲**The Shambles**—This is the most colorful old York street and the half-timbered core of town. Between there, the Minster and Monk Bar, it's a window shopper's delight.

▲▲▲**York Castle Museum**—Truly one of Europe's top museums, this is a walk with Dickens, the closest thing to a time-tunnel experience you'll ever have. It includes a magnificent collection of old shops well-stocked exactly as they were 150 years ago, costumes, armor, and the "every home needs one" exhibit, showing the evolution of vacuum cleaners, toilets, TVs, bicycles, stoves, etc. from their crude beginnings to now. Cafeteria, shop, car park, open daily 9:30-6:30, Sundays, 10:00-6:30, £2. Tel. 53611.

▲▲**Jorvik**—The new museum of Viking York takes you back 1,000 years—literally backwards—in a little Disney-type train car. Then, still seated, you cruise slowly through the sounds, sights, and even smells of the recreated Viking village of Jorvik. Next you tour the actual excavation sight (the best Viking find anywhere) and finally are let off to browse through a gallery of Viking shoes, combs, locks, and other intimate glimpses of their culture. Located on Coppergate, open daily 9:00-7:00; November-March 9:00-5:30, tel. 643211, £2. To minimize time in line—which can be an hour—go early or late.

DAY 22
YORK—CAMBRIDGE—LONDON

On our final day, we'll drive to Cambridge, and probably turn in our rental car. We'll tour and then savor this historic town, with its famous universities and lovely river. After dinner we'll take a quick train ride back to London where we complete our circle of Britain by returning to our hotel of three weeks ago.

Suggested Schedule	
9:00	Leave York, drive south.
12:00	Arrive Cambridge, leave bags at train station, turn in car, book walking tour at T.I., have lunch.
2:15	Walking Tour.
4:15	Free to explore, stroll through Backs, shop in center, go punting, or take a quick look at the Fitzwilliam Museum paintings.
7:00, 8:14 or 9:50	Catch the 70-minute train ride to London (confirm those times at the station). Tube or taxi to your London hotel. Tour over. Everybody off the bus!

Transportation
York to Cambridge—Cambridge is a three-hour drive from York. York is such a mess, you'll want to ask at your B&B for the best way to get to A19 south to Selby. At Selby, cut west on A63 to A1 and follow A1 all the way south to Cambridge. There is a tempting motorway (171) further west, but stick to the A1 which is near motorway quality and a more interesting drive. Finally, come into Cambridge on the A604, following the signs to the town center and then to the Tourist Info or Market Place. Driving in Cambridge is another headache. If you need to park, the huge, central Lyon Parking Lot is best.

    Cambridge to London—From Cambridge, if you're driving to London, any major road going west or south will direct you to the M11 motorway. It's 60 high speed miles (with no gas stations) to the London ring road. Needless to say, driving in London is no fun. Be sure to catch the poorly marked M25 outer ring road (you'll see Heathrow and Gatwick signs) and circle around to the best position to start your central attack. (You can buy a good London map at the Cambridge T.I., 40p.) If you do decide to drive into London—where your car is a useless headache—you'll learn why I recommend. . .

    Leaving Your Car in Cambridge—Ideally, you picked up a car at Heathrow that can be dropped at Cambridge. Hertz (Willhire Limited, 41 High St., Chesterton, tel. 68888), Budget (303 Newmarket Road, 323838), Kenning (47 Coldhams Lane, 61538), Avis (243 Mill Road, 212551), and Godfrey Davis (315 Mill Road, 248198). All the major rental agencies allow you to pick up in Heathrow and drop in Cambridge.

    With this plan, you'll drive to the Cambridge train station to check your bags and buy your London ticket, then drop your empty car off at the appropriate agency (see map). From there, take a taxi or one of many Market Square buses to the T.I. to get info and catch the city walk.

After dinner (or during dinner) the train will take you to London's Liverpool Street Station (hourly, £7, 70 minutes). Hop on London's handy Central subway line, and return to the hotel you reserved and paid for three weeks earlier.

Cambridge

60 miles north of London, this historic town of 100,000 people is world-famous for it prestigious university. Wordsworth, Isaac Newton, Tennyson, Darwin, and Prince Charles are a few products of this busy brainworks. Much more pleasant than its rival, Oxford, Cambridge is the epitome of a university town, with busy bikers, stately halls of residence, plenty of bookshops, and a fun youthfulness permeating its old walls.

Orientation

There's basically one main street separated from the river by the most interesting colleges. The town center has a handy T.I., colorful marketplace and a much needed huge parking lot. Everything is a pleasant walk away. Use the Tourist Info (Wheeler St., tel. 0223/322640, open Monday-Friday, 9:00-6:00; Saturday, 9:00-5:00; Sundays in summer, 10:30-3:30, good room-finding service). Remember, the university dominates —and owns—most of Cambridge. Sightseeing is a bit limited during the school term. Approximate term schedule is: January 15-March 15, April 15-June 8, October 8-December 8.

Sightseeing Highlights

▲▲**Walking Tour of the Colleges**—The best way to understand Cambridge's town-gown rivalry and be sure to get a good rundown on the historic and scenic highlights of the university—as well as some fun local gossip—is to take the walking tour. It leaves from the T.I. at 11:00, 1:00, 2:00 and 3:00 in the summer (11:00 and 2:00 off season), £2. Buy tickets or call in reservations as early that day as you can. If you miss a tour or want your own, private guides are usually on call charging £15 for the two-hour walk. These tours do their best to work in King's College Chapel and Trinity's Wren Library.

▲▲▲**King's College Chapel**—The most impressive single building in town, high Gothic at its best, incredible fan vaulting and Rubens' great Adoration of the Magi. Open 9:30-5:45 daily.

▲▲**Trinity College**—The richest and biggest college here, don't miss its great courtyard or the Wren library with its wonderful carving and fascinating manuscripts. Unfortunately, it's only open Monday-Friday, 12:00-2:00.

▲▲**Fitzwilliam Museum**—The best museum of antiquities and art outside of London. Fine Impressionist paintings, old manuscripts, Greek, Egyptian, and Mesopotamian collections. Antiquities open 10:00-2:00, Paintings, 2:00-5:00, everything on Sunday, 2:15-5:00, closed Monday. Free and actually fun.

Punting on the Cam—For a little levity and probably more exercise than you really want, try hiring one of the traditional flat-bottom punts from stalls near either bridge and pole yourself up and down (around and around, more likely), the lazy Cam. Once you get the hang of it, it's a fine way to enjoy the scenic side of Cambridge. After 5:00 it's less crowded.

Accommodations

If you decide to spend the night in Cambridge, you'll be arriving early enough to find a room through the tourist office.

Youth Hostel—The Cambridge hostel is modern, easy-going, friendly, clean, and located near the train station, a 20-minute walk from the center. Tel. 354601, at 97 Tenison Road.

May View Guest House—Perfectly located just off the heavenly Jesus Green and three minutes from downtown. £8—£10 per person, 12 Park Parade, CB5-8AL, tel, 66018.

There are several B&Bs on Jesus Lane (call 60648, 356961, or 353858). Otherwise, most places are farther out in the Chesterton Road area.

Itinerary Options

Cambridge is a very easy day trip from London—about an hour each way, round trip rates costing only a little more than one way (£7.)

Post-Tour London

■ Remember to call your airline to reconfirm your return flight three days in advance, leaving your hotel's phone number for any messages.
■ Hopefully you will have thought ahead, taking advantage of the op-

portunity to reserve hard-to-get tickets at the start of the trip to enjoy a special show or event before returning home.

■ Ask at your hotel for the easiest way to the airport. To Gatwick, take the shuttle train from Victoria Station. To Heathrow, take the subway or the Airbus. Airbus is easiest, dropping you right at terminal 3 for international departures (£3). Taxis are a ripoff from airports, but two or three people in a hurry can ride reasonably from the West End out. I flagged down a cab while waiting for the Airbus and negotiated a £10 ride from Holland Park to Heathrow.

■ Call before going out to the airport to check for delays.

■ Call home (50p or a pound is enough) to say all's well and what time you're due in.

■ Remember, you'll arrive home at almost the same time you leave London, considering the hours you gain in flight.

POST-TOUR OPTION: IRELAND

The obvious gap in this 22-day plan is Ireland. I agonized over what to do with the friendly Emerald Isle. I love Ireland. Most who visit do. But it doesn't make it into the top 22 days. Still, Ireland is easy to work in as a side trip or finale to this 22-day plan. Here are a few points to consider.

Itinerary Strategy—Getting There

Ireland can be inserted into the 22-day plan from North Wales. Boats sail from Holyhead to Dun Laoghaire three or four times a day (3½ hour trip, $35, get ticket ASAP in London). Ask about cheap round trip tickets. The train/boat London—Dublin ride costs about $60, overnight or all day. Buses go daily between Glasgow and Belfast (10-12 hours, $25).

Consider an "open-jaws" flight plan, flying into London and home from Shannon Airport in Western Ireland. Your 22-day itinerary then would be: London, Wales, England, Scotland, Belfast, Dublin, West Ireland, fly home.

If you'll be touring the Continent with a Eurail pass, start it in Ireland (it's good on Irish trains and many buses) and ride free on the otherwise expensive 24-hour boat ride to France. (Note: This ride can be rough. Upon boarding, those concerned about seasickness should go straight to the ship's cafeteria and eat a small plastic tub full of strawberry jelly. While this won't stop the nausea, it helps the aftertaste).

Transportation in Ireland

For a quick visit to Dublin and a day tour into the countryside you'll just ride the boat and catch a bus tour in Dublin. For a more extensive visit, here are your options. Irish trains are expensive and not extensive, with meager schedules and coverage. Britrail Passes don't work here. The bus is cheaper with better coverage. Study special passes; students get a 50% discount with ISIC cards. Taking a car from England is complicated and expensive. Most people rent a separate car (by the week) from the USA for Ireland. Hitchhiking is the best in Europe, very safe. You'll make more friends, spend less money.

Sightseeing Highlights

Dublin—Not a favorite city of mine but worth a day. Compact center around O'Connell Street Bridge and the River Liffy. Boats land at nearby Dun Laoghaire with good bus connections into Dublin. Tourist Info at 14 Upper O'Connell Street, tel 747733, open Monday-Saturday 8:30-6:00, has good room-finding services. Orient yourself with a city walking tour.

Visit Trinity College (stately grounds, historic buildings, illuminated Book of Kells manuscript); the National Museum (moving Nathan-Hale type patriotism of the martyrs of the 1916 Rebellion, impressive medieval and earlier Irish artifacts open Tuesday-Saturday 10:00-5:00, Sunday 2:00-5:00); General Post Office (unimpressive building but it's the site of the 1916 proclamation of the Independent Irish Republic); Kilmainham Jail (symbol of the Irish struggle against Britain, martyr memorabilia, open Wednesday 10:00-12:00, 2:30-4:00, and Sunday

3:00-5:00 only); Guinness Brewery (video show, free beer, Monday-Friday 10:00-3:00).

For entertainment, sample the great Irish theater (Abbey Theater and many others, shows Monday-Saturday at 8:00pm), seek out some Irish folk music in a local pub, or check out some Irish sports—hurling (the rugged national sport that's like airborne hockey), or Gaelic football (a violent form of rugby). Games nearly every Sunday at Dublin's Croke Park. Use the periodical entertainment guide called "In Dublin" for music, theater, sports and tour listings.

Glendalough—The best short day trip from Dublin for a sample of rural Ireland is into the Wicklow mountains to Glendalough. 1,500 years ago the hermit St. Kevin established a thriving monastic school here. Today its ruins surrounded by scenic forests and lakes are understandably popular with tourists. Look into a one-day tour with a local company.

Belfast—Just a direct three-hour trainride north, this embattled capital of the North offers a safe and fascinating look at "The Troubles." You'll be frisked at the checkpoint and then step into the traffic-free "safe zone." Browse through a bomb damage clearance sale. Take a side trip south to the wonderful Cultra Open Air Folk Museum, talk to the people. With common sense (don't sing Catholic songs in Protestant pubs), Belfast is as safe as London. See the chapter on Belfast in *Europe Through the Back Door*. Consider a Belfast-Glasgow bus connection.

Wexford-Rosslare Harbor—Visit this area only to catch the boat to South Wales or France.

Cork—Ireland's rough, but pleasant, second city. Boat to France (free on Eurail pass) and near the famous Blarney Castle with its too-famous Blarney Stone (that hordes of Americans kiss to get the "gift of gab.")

Cashel—A stirring religious and political center from the mysterious days of St. Patrick. Fine Celtic cross graveyard, good tours, open daily 9:00-7:30, 10:30-4:30 in winter. Two buses a day to and from Dublin and Cork.

Dingle Peninsula—My favorite scenery in the British Isles is Ireland's West Coast. And the best in the West is the rugged beauty of hearty Dingle Peninsula—just north of the very touristy Ring of Kerry. Dingle is a Gaeltacht—a region where the locals still speak the old Irish or Gaelic language. This is a cultural preserve with traditional dress, music, and lifestyles complementing the natural beauty. (See *Europe Through the Back Door* chapter on Dingle). Train to the pleasant town of Tralee, then bus or thumb to Dingle town. Set up at Mrs. Farrell's Corner House (tel. 066/51516). Rent a bike for the circular trip out to Slea Head (closest point to America, incredibly scenery, villages, explore the medieval monks' stone beehive huts, or clochans, along the way) but be home in time to catch the nightly folk music at O'Flaherty's Pub.

Galway—Largest city in the west. Cozy, historic, 3½ hours by train to and from Dublin and Cork, direct bus to Rosslare. Daily boats and cheap flights to the Aran Islands (try for any kind of discount you can dream up).

Aran Islands—Off the coast of Galway, this tiny group of wave-whipped islands is a stark and traditional outpost of Irish culture and is not terribly touristy. Spend two days on the main island, rent bikes and explore. Boats connect islands with the mainland. One goes to Doolin, home of Ireland's best folk music —but not much else.

Donegal—Ireland in the extreme, the cultural Yukon of this lush island where everyone seems to be typecast for an Irish movie. Enter Donegal with caution, for while it has no real "sights," it is seductive and many unwary visitors end up skipping the rest of their itinerary. One Arizona accountant "called in well" and was never seen again.

Helpful Hints

Understand Ireland's "Troubles"—the North-South, Catholic-Protestant problem. A fine background and wonderful reading is *Trinity* by Leon Uris.

Ireland is very small (about 150 by 200 miles) but it has no English-style motorways. Transportation is slow. Approach every trip as a joyride. Traveling in Ireland is generally cheaper than in England. Ireland's pound is worth just over a dollar—much less than the British pound.

The Irish B&Bs are even cozier and less expensive than England's, and traveling without reservations is not difficult. Use the *Let's Go: Britain and Ireland* guidebook.

You'll find that Ireland's weather ranges from damp to drizzly to downpour and her people are her main attraction. You can't enjoy Ireland without enjoying her people.

Suggested Itinerary

Quick Ireland, spliced in from North Wales:

Day 1	Leave rental car at Holyhead, take boat to Dun Laoghaire, set up in Dublin.
Day 2	Sightsee Dublin.
Day 3	Sidetrip south to Glendalough and Wicklow Mountains.
Day 4	Early boat back to Holyhead, pick up car or train, and go to Blackpool.

Longer Ireland:

	Revise your 22-day plan as if returning to London on the overnight train from Scotland, (London-Bath-North Wales-York-Edinburgh). Turn in car in Edinburgh if driving.
Day 21	Edinburgh—Glasgow—Bus/Boat—Belfast.
Day 22	Sightsee in Belfast, afternoon at Cultra Folk Museum.
Day 23	Early train to Dublin, sightsee all day there.
Day 24	Dublin—Cashel—Tralee—Dingle.
Day 25	Dingle, bike the peninsula.
Day 26	Dingle—Tralee—Shannon Airport to fly home; or, Dingle—Dublin, and night train/boat back to London.

PRACTICAL EXTRAS

Sleeping in Britain

Thank God Britain has such lousy hotels. Because the alternative—bed and breakfast places—is second-to-none, with a homey charm that I'd prefer to even the most luxurious European hotels. Generally, the less atmosphere a hotel has, the more it charges. But guesthouses and bed and breakfasts seem to be popping up all over the place to fill that void.

On this trip I'm assuming you have a reasonable but limited budget. Skip hotels. Go the B&B (bed and breakfast) way. Where there's a demand, there will be a supply. B&Bs hang out their shingle where you need them, and any town with tourists has a tourist office that can book one for you or give you a list and point you in the right direction. Without a T.I. (Tourist Information office), ask people on the street for help.

B&Bs are family run, usually just a large home with a few extra rooms to let. They charge from $10—$15 and always include the "full English breakfast". How much coziness and extra tea and biscuits is tossed in varies tremendously.

The B&Bs I've recommended are nearly all stocking-feet comfortable and very "homely," as they say in England. My prerequisites for recommending a place are: friendly; in a central, safe, quiet neighborhood; clean, with good beds, a sink in the room and shower down the hall; not in other guidebooks and therefore filled mostly by English travelers, and willing to hold a room until 4:00—6:00 pm without a deposit. (In certain cases my recommendations don't meet all these prerequisites.)

I promised the owners of the places I list that you would be reliable when you make a telephone reservation—please don't let these people (or me) down. If you'll be delayed or won't make it, call in. They can normally fill your bed only with the help of the local tourist office room-finding service which usually closes at 5:00 or 6:00. Americans are notorious for "standing up" B&Bs.

A few tips: B&B proprietors are selective in who they invite in for the night. Risky-looking people find many places suddenly full. If you'll be staying for more than one night you are a "desirable". Sometimes staying several nights earns you a better price—ask about it. The T.I. generally takes about a 10% commission for those they send. If you book direct, the B&B gets it all. Nearly all B&Bs have plenty of stairs. Expect good exercise and be happy you packed light. If one B&B is full, ask for guidance. (Mention this book . . .). Owners usually work together and can call up an ally to land you a bed. Unless I'm relying on a particular recommendation, I enjoy shopping for my B&B, touring three places and choosing the best. "Twin" and "double" are two entirely different things. If you'll take two single beds or a double bed say so or you may be needlessly turned away. B&Bs advertise with prominent signs in their yard or windows.

Room-finding is very easy from Sept. 15 to June 1st. Otherwise call ahead, try to arrive early and take advantage of room-finding services in most tourist offices. They charge about a pound for reservations in another city but can save you lots of headaches.

Youth Hostels: Britain has four hundred youth hostels—of all shapes and sizes. They can be historic castles or depressing huts, serene

and comfy or overrun by noisy children, but they're never expensive.
Hostels charge less than $5 a night and normally provide hot meals at
budget prices and a member's kitchen for even cheaper eating. They are
generally wonderfully located and pleasantly run, but hostels are not
B&Bs. You need a membership card (available in the US or in Britain),
there's a dorm for men and one for women. They lock up through mid-
day and usually at 11:00 pm. Big city hostels are normally more chaotic
and less comfortable then town and country ones. Off-season hosteling
is easy and so uncrowded that married couples can often share a room.
In peak season, most hostels fill up by dinnertime. There is absolutely
no age limit to hosteling. In fact, there's a new card giving youth
hostelers over the age of sixty a discount. Many English hostelers have
been at it for 50 years. Use the British hostel guidebook, available at any
hostel. If you're traveling alone, this is the best way to defeat hotel lone-
liness. Hostels are also a tremendous source of local and budget travel
information. If you hostel selectively you'll enjoy historical and very interesting buildings.

Eating in Britain (Those Who Do Have a Better Trip)
I think English food is just fine. But then, I liked dorm food, too. True,
England isn't famous for its cuisine and it probably never will be, but
we tourists have to eat. And, if there's any good place to cut corners to
stretch your budget in Britain, it's in eating. Here are a few tips on
budget eating in Britain.
The English (or Scottish or Welsh) "fry" is famous as a hearty way to
start the day. Also known as a "plate of cardiac arrest," the breakfast is
especially feasty if you've just come from the lands of the skimpy con-
tinental breakfast across the Channel.
The standard B&B breakfast starts with juice and cereal (or porridge).
Top-notch places give both and occasionally even grapefruit sections.
Try Weatibix, an English cousin of shredded wheat. Scotland serves
great porridge. Then, with tea or coffee, you get a heated plate with a
fried egg, very lean Canadian-style bacon, a pretty bad sausage, a grilled
tomato, and often a slice of delightfully greasy pan toast and sauteed
mushrooms. The last course is a rack of toast with butter and mar-
melade. This meal tides many travelers over until dinner.
One problem with B&Bs and this itinerary is that many don't serve
until 8:30 or 9:00. If you need an early start, ask politely if it's possible.
Consider skipping breakfast on occasion if a quick start is important.
For lunch on this tour I'd picnic. Restaurants cost too much time and
money. Outfit your car with a backseat cardboard pantry. Our standard
shopping list includes: boxes of orange juice (Del Monte is best), fresh
bread, tasty English cheese, meat, a tube of Colman's English mustard,
local eatin' apples, bananas, small tomatoes, chocolate-covered "Diges-
tive Biscuits," rice crackers, gorp or nuts, paper towels, and any local
specialties we bump into. English open-air markets and supermarkets
are fine. We often eat "meals on wheels" en route to save 30 precious
minutes and enjoy a relaxed-paced meal as we drive. A small plastic
water bottle, zip-lock baggies and a Swiss army knife are handy.
Pub Grub—Pubs offer the best basic budget dinner in friendly sur-
roundings. Pubs generally serve assorted meat pies (steak and kidney

pie, shepherd's pie, etc.), curried dishes, fish, quiche and vegetables—
invariably chips and peas. Servings are hearty, service is quick and
dinners cost from $2.50 to $5.00. Your pint of beer or cider adds another dollar. Free water is always available. A "ploughman's lunch" is a
modern "traditional" English meal that nearly every tourist tries. . .
once.

Beer—The British take great pride in their beer. They think that
drinking beer cold and carbonated as Americans do ruins the taste. To
the average American, a good English beer tastes flat, smooth and room
temperature. Experiment with the English "bitters," ales and local
brews. Stick to whatever's on tap and try the draft cider. . . cautiously.
And, when you just want a good cold and unexotic beer like you get at
home, ask for a lager.

Pub hours vary, but they are usually open 11:00—3:00 and 5:30—
11:00 pm. Drinks are served by the pint or the half-pint (not macho for
a man to order just a half). Teetotallers can order soft drinks or a
"shandy." "Pub" is short for "public house"—go there to be social.
They're the next best thing to relatives in every town.

Other Budget Meals—While English restaurants are fairly expensive, there are plenty of cheap alternatives: fish 'n chips joints, Chinese
take-outs, cafeterias, B&Bs that serve evening meals, and your typical
good old "greasy spoon" places. Throughout Britain I've had very good
luck following the recommendations of my B&Bs.

Money
The British "Pound Sterling" (£) is broken into 100 "pence" (p). A
pound or "quid" is worth about $1.50. Pence means "cents" and is
usually called just "p." You'll find coins ranging from one pence to one
pound and bills from one pound to fifty. Shillings, a confusing leftover
from England's pre-decimal days, are worth five pence, two shillings is
ten pence.

To figure pounds into dollars, just multiply the British prices by 1.5.
For example, £6 = $9, £4.50 = $6.75 and 80p = $1.20. Get used to
this formula as soon as possible. (The actual exchange rate floats.
Whether its 1.43 or 1.52, just keep it a simple 1.5.)

Scotland and Ireland have their own currencies. English and Scottish
money are worth the same and are good in both countries (but it can be
troublesome to spend Scottish currency in England). The Irish-English
money relationship is like the Canadian-American one. English money
is a little more valuable. Treat Ireland as a different country (which it is).

Britain has a 15% sales tax that is called a "value added tax," or "VAT".
This is built into nearly everything you buy. Tourists can get a refund on
this VAT on souvenirs they take out of the country but it's a major headache. Unless you buy something worth several hundred dollars, your refund won't be worth the delays, incidental expenses, and headaches
that complicate the lives of TISVATR (Tourists In Search of VAT
Refunds).

Even in jolly old England you should use traveler's checks and a
money belt. Theft is a part of tourism and the meek may be blessed but
the careless are sitting ducks. A moneybelt is peace of mind.

If you'll be traveling exclusively in Great Britain, buy traveler's checks in pounds sterling. If you get Barclays checks you'll find a Barclays Bank in nearly every English town, sometimes avoiding the dollar or more commission banks charge for changing money. I bring a credit card only because it's necessary to rent a car. Spend cash—not plastic—as you travel. Save time and money by changing plenty of money at a time. With a money belt you can carry several hundred pounds (worth of money) safely. For money belts see our catalog at the back of the book.

Americans have an easy time in Britain with weights and measures. Like us, the British use Fahrenheit, miles, inches, pounds and ounces.

Driving British

Driving in Britain is basically wonderful—once you remember to stay on the left and after you've mastered the "round-abouts". It's really very easy if you want it to be. Here are a few random tips:

Your US licence is all you need. An AA membership (like our AAA, not our AA) comes with most rentals. Be sure you know how it works. Gas is about $3 per gallon and self-serve. Know what octane rating your car takes, push the correct button and pump away. (Over 3,000 miles on my last trip I paid 8 cents per mile for gas.) Seatbelts are required by law in the front seat.

Speed limits are 30 mph in town, 70 on the motorways and "dual carriageways" and 60 elsewhere. Don't tell anyone, but I drove ten to twenty miles over the limit for six weeks and was never stopped. (Time estimates in this book assume a law-abiding speed, however.) Avoid big cities whenever possible. Most have modern ring roads to skirt the congestion. Rush hours are basically the same as ours. The shortest distance between any two points is almost always the motorway.

Parking is confusing. One yellow line means no parking Monday—Saturday during work hours. Double yellow lines mean no parking ever. Broken yellow means short stops are okay, but always look for explicit signs or ask a passing passerby. (Don't tell anybody this either, but I've gotten a few parking tickets in my day and have enjoyed a healthy measure of "tourist's immunity.")

Copy your car key as soon as possible so you won't get locked out and so your partner enjoys access to the car. Buy some windex to clean your windows each morning. If you want other drivers to give you a wide berth, pick up a red "L" sign at a hardware store. Display it on the back of your car and you'll be feared like any "Learner" should be.

Great Britain in 22 Days—by Train and Bus

Britain has a great train and bus system, and travelers who don't want to (or can't afford to) drive a rental car can enjoy 22 exciting days using public transportation. But you'll lose a lot of control, and travel in Britain, more than in any other European country, lends itself to car travel.

A train/bus trip requires some tailoring to avoid areas that are difficult without your own wheels and to take advantage of certain bonuses train travel offers. Consider a plan like this:

Britain by Train in 22 Days	
Day 1	Arrive in London
Day 2	London
Day 3	London
Day 4	Bath
Day 5	Side trip to Wells and Glastonbury
Day 6	Cardiff, St Fagans, to Cheltenham
Day 7	Explore Cotswolds with Cheltenham as a base
Day 8	Stratford, Warwick
Day 9	Coventry to North Wales
Day 10	North Wales
Day 11	North Wales—Blackpool
Day 12	Blackpool—York
Day 13	York
Day 14	York—Durham—Hadrian's Wall—Edinburgh
Day 15	Edinburgh
Day 16	Edinburgh
Day 17	Edinburgh—Mallaig
Day 18	Isle of Skye—Inverness, night train to London
Day 19	London—side trip to Cambridge
Day 20	Side trip from London to Salisbury, Stonehenge
Day 21	Free day
Day 22	Free day to insert where needed

London is the hub, with speedy commutor trains going everywhere. Remember, London has many stations, each serving a general region. Round-trip "day return" tickets are just a bit more than one-way fares, making day-trips to places like Cambridge, Salisbury, Stonehenge, Oxford, Stratford and Bath reasonable. **London to Salisbury** (80 miles from Waterloo Station, 90 minutes, hourly), **Salisbury to Stonehenge** (9 miles, 30 minutes bus ride changing at Amesbury, several a day from downtown or station), **London to Bath** (from Paddington Station, 90 minutes, hourly). Note: All times and schedules listed in this chapter work the same in both directions.

Bath—Most larger journeys change at Bristol (15 minutes from Bath, four times an hour).

Bristol to Cardiff (60 minutes, hourly). Bath RR info—63075, coach info—64446.

Cardiff—The transportation hub of south Wales. Buses direct to St. Fagan's and Caerphilly. Train to Cheltenham (80 minutes, every two hours). RR info—28000, bus info—371331.

Cheltenham—The Cotswolds are hiking, biking or driving country but a few train lines and sporadic bus service will get you around if necessary. Cheltenham, from a public transportation point of view, is your best home base. Be sure to pick up the "Cotswold Bus and Rail Guide" there. **Cheltenham—Birmingham** (hourly, 45 minutes rides). Train info—29501, bus info—22021, Cheltenham tourist info—522878.

Stratford—Warwick—Coventry—This segment of the trip is so easy by car but messy otherwise. Birmingham is the transportation hub of this region and each place is well served from Birmingham. **Stratford to Warwick** (train and bus almost hourly, 20 minute ride), **to Coventry** (bus almost hourly, 75-minute ride), **to London** (8 trains a day, 2¼ hours), Train info—204444, bus info—204181. Tour companies make day tripping from Stratford to Blenheim, Oxford, Cotswolds, Warwick and Coventry possible—but not cheap. **Coventry**—Bus 25 connects the bus and train stations going through the center of town past the cathedral and tourist info. National Express (tel. 730-0202) offers 12-hour day trips from London to Coventry and Warwick for £10.

Iron Bridge Gorge—This birthplace of the Industrial Revolution is still in the Stone Age, transportation-wise. It's too difficult without a car and, for most, not worth the trouble.

North Wales—The plan in this book won't work without a car but North Wales has good and scenic trains and buses. You can pick up plenty of info locally and a special "Day Rover" ticket gives you a day of buses for only £2. **Chester—Holyhead** train (6-8 times a day, two hours). **Caenarfon—Blaenau Ffestiniog** (bus every two hours). Look into the old miniature-gauge Ffestiniog railroad.

Chester—Crew—Preston—Blackpool. This is England's industrial heartland, and trains are very frequent. With the two changes, this journey should take three hours.

Blackpool—Manchester (two per hour, 90-minute ride).

Manchester—York (leaving at 28 past each hour, 90 minute ride).

Lakes District is frustrating for those with limited time and no car. There are buses and trains serving the area, but I'd skip it.

York and **Edinburgh** are very well connected by train (hourly trips, three hours). That train stops in Durham and Newcastle. York-London (hourly, two hours long). Train info 25671, bus info 24161.

Durham—Newcastle (Four trains per hour, 15 minutes). Tour Hadrian's Wall from Newcastle. The Newcastle —Carlisle train is very scenic, stopping at Hexham and Haltwhistle and going right along the wall (hourly, 90 minute ride). In the summer there's a tourist-oriented bus service four times a day from Newcastle.

Edinburgh—To get to the rugged west and islands from Edinburgh you go via **Glasgow** (trains from Edinburgh twice an hour, 50 minutes) or **Inverness** four times a day, 3½ hours). Edinburgh has plenty of reasonably priced organized bus tours covering Loch Ness, Oban, Isle of Mull and Inverness. **Glasgow—Oban train** (3 hours, three a day), **Glasgow—Malliag** (6 hours with an hour break in Fort William, three a day), **Kyle of Lockalsh—Inverness** (2 ½ hours, three a day). Edinburgh train info—556-2451, bus info—556-8464.

Overnight train back to London: **Inverness—London** (19:30—6:47, 20:30—7:32 each night), a sleeping berth is a good investment. Inverness train info—232651, bus info—233371.

A trip of this. . . ferocity. . . justifies a BritRail Pass. These passes give you unlimited rail travel in England, Scotland and Wales. You must buy it outside of Great Britain (ideally, from your travel agent). The promotional info is a bit complicated, but very thorough. Read it carefully.

1986 BritRail Pass prices are:

	7 days	14 days	21 days	1 month
Youth (under 26)	$ 95	$150	$190	$225
Economy	115	175	220	260
First Class	155	230	290	335
Senior First Class (over 60)	115	175	220	260

For more info, including British Rail network map, write to your nearest BritRail Travel International Office:
- 630 Third Ave., New York, NY 10017, (212)-599-5400
- 510 West Sixth St., Los Angeles, CA 90014, (213)-626-0088
- 333 N. Michigan Ave., Chicago, IL 60601, (312)-263-1910
- Plaza of the Americas, North Tower, Suite 750, Dallas, TX 75021, (214)-748-0860
- 94 Cumberland Street, Suite 601, Toronto M5R 1A3, ON, (416)-929-3333
- 409 Granville Street, Vancouver V6C 1T2, BC, (604)-683-6896

British buses are cheaper but slower than trains. They will take you where the trains don't. Stations are often at or near train stations. The British distinguish between "buses" (for local runs with lots of stops) and "coaches" (long distance, express runs). If your budget is very tight, you can save plenty by skipping the BritRail Pass in favor of the Brit-Express Pass which gives you unlimited travel on the National Express buses (15 days for about $80, 22 days for about $100, through your travel agent or in London—tel. 730-0202).

Of course you could do this whole trip hitchhiking. It would take more time but you'd make a lot more friends. If you plan to ride your thumb get a hitching guidebook (try *Hitch Hikers Manual: Britain*, £3.95, from Vacation Work, 9 Park End St. Oxford OX1 IHJ, or *A Hitchhiker's Guide to Great Britain*, by Penguin, £2.95).

Getting to London—Fly!
Flying to London is your major expense, and a little study can save you a bundle. Fares and regulations to England vary all over the USA. From the East Coast you can fly cheapest by studying the New York Times travel section and comparing standby, Peoples, and cut-rate prices with the best deal your travel agent can give you. From the West Coast you

can't beat what a good travel agent will sell you. You need an agent who knows and enjoys budget European travel. Read the newspapers, talk to other travelers, but most of all establish a loyal relationship with a good agent. London is about the cheapest European destination from the States, and if you can avoid summer travel it's even cheaper.

The "Open to View" ticket
Born and raised in a society like ours, we jump on special coupons, all-you-can-eat meals and clever gimmicks that sound so good. After your plane ticket, BritRail Pass, and car rental (which is much cheaper from the States) nearly anything you buy in the USA is a bad deal that will do more complicating than simplifing.

This is also true for the "Open To View" ticket, which gives you free entry for a month to hundreds of Britain's top sights. It costs $32 in the States and £16 (or $23) in the U.K. Don't buy it until you get to London. The Heathrow and Victoria station tourist offices issue them on the spot.

On this 22-day plan, the OTV covers: Tower of London (£3), Stonehenge (£1), Tintern Abbey (90p), Blenheim Palace (£2), Warwick Castle (£3.25), Caenarfon Castle (£1.60), Urquhart Castle (£1), Culloden (£1), Edinburgh Castle (£2), Georgian House (£1), Gladstones Land (£1), Housteads Roman Fort (£1), Roman Baths in Bath (£1), Holyrood Palace (£1), and several other sights you may see. Total value—£22, your cost £16—and you only feel the pain once. Get it.

Festivals
Jousting Tournament of Knights, last Sun & Mon in May at Chilham Castle near Canterbury, Medieval pageantry, colorful.
Allington Castle Medieval Market, 2nd or 3rd Sat in June in Maidstone (30 mi. SE of London). Medieval crafts and entertainment.
Druid Summer Solstice Ceremonies, June 20 or 21, Stonehenge. Hoods and white robes, rituals from midnight to sunrise at about 4:45am.
Ainwick Medieval Fair, last Sun in June to next Sat. Medieval costumes, competition, entertainment. Ainwick, 30 mi. N. of Newcastle.
Haslemere Early Music Festival, 2 Fridays before 4th Sat in July. 16th-18th c. music on original instruments. 40 mi. S. of London.
Sidmouth International Folklore Festival, 1st to 2nd Fridays in August, 300 events, 15 mi. E. of Exeter.
Reading Rock Festival, last weekend of August. England's best. 40 mi. W of London.
Nottingham Goose Fair, 1st Thurs-Sat in Oct, one of England's oldest and largest fairs. Nottingham.
Guy Fawkes Day, Nov. 5. Nationwide holiday.

CULTURAL INSIGHTS FOR TRAVELERS

What's So Great About Britain?

Regardless of any revolution we had 200 years ago, Americans "go home" to Britain. This most popular tourist destination has a strange influence and power over us.

Britain is small—about the size of Uganda (or Idaho)—600 miles tall and 300 at its widest. Its highest mountain is 4,400 feet—a foothill by our standards—the population is a quarter of the USA's and, politically and economically, the Great Britain closing out the 20th century is only a weak shadow of the days when it boasted, "The sun never sets on the British Empire."

At one time Britain owned one-fifth of the world and accounted for over half the planet's industrial output. Today the Empire is down to tidbits like the Falklands and Northern Ireland, and her industrial production is 7% of the world's total.

Still, Britain is a world leader. Her heritage, her culture and her people cannot be measured in traditional units of power.

Great Britain is a union of four countries—England, Wales, Scotland and Northern Ireland. Cynics call it an English Empire ruled by London, and there is some tension between the dominant Anglo-Saxon English (46 million) and their Celtic brothers (10 million).

In the Dark Ages, the Angles moved into this region from Europe pushing the Celtic inhabitants to the undesirable fringe of the islands. The Angles settled in Angle-land (England) while the Celts made do in Wales, Scotland and Ireland.

Today Wales, with 2½ million people, struggles along with a terrible economy, dragged down by the depressed mining industry. There is a great deal of Welsh pride apparent in the local music and in the bilingual signs. 500,000 people speak the Welsh language.

Scotland is big, taking up one-third of Britain, but is sparsely inhabited by only 5½ million people. Only about 80,000 speak old Scottish but the Scots enjoy a large measure of autonomy with their separate Church of Scotland, their own legal system and Scottish currency. Scotland is allowed to pretty much run its own domestic affairs. Its economy is sagging, but the recent North Sea oil boom has been a great shot in the Scottish arm.

Ireland, the island west of England, is divided. Most of it is the completely independent and Catholic Republic of Ireland. The top quarter is Northern Ireland—ruled from London. Long ago the Protestant English and Scots moved into the north, the industrial heartland of Ireland, and told the Catholic Irish to "go to Hell or go to Connemara." They moved to the bleak and less productive parts of the island, and the seeds of today's "Troubles" were planted. There's no easy answer or easy blame, but that island has struggled—its population is only a third (3 million) of what it used to be—and the battle continues.

As a visitor today, you'll see a politically polarized England. The Conservatives, with Margaret Thatcher at the helm, are taking a Reaganesque approach to Britain's serious problems, returning to Victorian values—community, family, hard work, thrift and trickle-down. The Labor and Liberal parties see an almost irreparable break-up of the

social service programs so dear to them and so despised by the Conservatives.

British History For The Traveler
When Julius Caesar landed on the misty and mysterious isle of Britain in
55 BC, England entered the history books. The primitive Celtic tribes
he conquered were themselves invaders who had earlier conquered the
even more mysterious people who built Stonehenge in prehistoric
times.
   The Romans built towns and roads (including Icknield Way and Foss
Way which remain today) and established their capital at "Londinium."
The Celtic natives, consisting of "Gaels," "Picts" and "Scots," were not
subdued so easily in present-day Scotland and Wales, and the Romans
had to build Hadrian's Wall near the Scottish border to keep invading
Scots out. Even today, the Celtic language and influence are strongest in
the Gael-ic and Scot-tish regions.
   As Rome fell, so fell Roman Britain—a victim of invaders and internal
troubles. Barbarian tribes from Germany and Denmark called Angles
and Saxons swept through the southern part of the island, establishing
"Angle-land." These were the days of the real King Arthur, probably a
Christianized Roman general fighting valiantly but vainly against invading barbarians. The island was plunged into 500 years of Dark
Ages—wars, plagues, and poverty —lit only by the dim candle of a few
learned Christian monks and missionaries trying to convert the
barbarians.
   Modern England began with yet another invasion. William the Conquerer and his Norman troops crossed the Channel from France in
1066. He crowned himself king in Westminster Abbey (as all subsequent
royalty would) and began building the Tower of London. French-
speaking Norman kings ruled the country for two centuries.
   With their fall, the country suffered through two more centuries of
civil wars, with various noble families vying for the crown. In one of
the most bitter feuds, the York and Lancaster families fought the "War of
the Roses," so-called because of the white and red flowers they chose as
their symbols. Battles; intrigues; kings, nobles and ladies imprisoned
and executed in the Tower—it's a wonder the country survived its
rulers.
   The country was finally united by the "third-party" Tudor family.
Henry VIII, a Tudor, was England's Renaissance king. He was handsome,
athletic, a poet, a scholar and a musician. He was also arrogant, cruel,
gluttonous and paranoid. He went through six wives in forty years,
divorcing, imprisoning or beheading them when they no longer suited
his needs. Henry also "divorced" England from the Catholic Church, establishing the Protestant Church of England (Anglican Church) and setting in motion years of religious squabbles. Henry also "dissolved" the
monasteries, leaving just the shells of many formerly glorious abbeys
dotting the countryside.
   Henry's daughter, Queen Elizabeth I, made England a great naval and
trading power and presided over the "Elizabethan era" of great writers,
including Shakespeare.
   The long-standing quarrel between England's kings and nobles in

Parliament finally erupted into a Civil War (1650). Parliament forces under the Puritan farmer Oliver Cromwell defeated—and beheaded—King Charles I. This Civil War left its mark on much of what you'll see in England. Eventually, Parliament invited Charles' son to retake the throne. This Restoration of the monarchy was accompanied by a great rebuilding of London (including Christopher Wren's St. Paul's Cathedral), which had been devastated by the Great Fire of 1666.

Britain grew as a great naval power, colonizing and trading with all parts of the globe. Her naval superiority ("Britannia rules the waves") was secured by Admiral Nelson's victory over Napoleon's fleet at the Battle of Trafalgar while Lord Wellington (with his son Beef) stomped Napoleon on land at Waterloo. Nelson and Wellington are memorialized by many arches, columns, squares, etc. throughout England.

Economically, Britain led the world into the Industrial Age with her mills, factories, coal mines and trains. By the time of Queen Victoria's reign (1837—1901), Britain was at the zenith of power with a colonial empire that covered ⅕ of the world.

The Twentieth Century has not been kind to Britain, however. Two World Wars devastated the population. The Nazi "Blitz" reduced much of London to rubble. Her colonial empire has dwindled to almost nothing and the economy is plagued by strikes, inflation and unemployment. The "Irish Troubles" are a constant thorn as the Catholic inhabitants of British-ruled Northern Ireland fight for the same independence their southern neighbors won decades ago.

The tradition of greatness continues unbowed, however, presided over by Queen Elizabeth II, her husband Prince Phillip, the heir-apparent Prince Charles and his wife, Lady Di.

Architecture in Britain
From Stonehenge to Big Ben, travelers are going to be storming castle walls, climbing spiral staircases and snapping the pictures of 5,000 years of architecture. Let's sort it out.

The oldest stuff—mysterious and prehistoric—goes from before Roman times back to 3,000 B.C. The earliest—like Stonehenge and Avebury—is from the Stone and Bronze Ages. The remains from this period are made of huge stones or mounds of earth, even manmade hills, and were built for worship or burial. Iron Age people (600 BC—400 AD) left us desolate stone forts.

The Romans thrived in Britain from 50—400 A.D. building cities, walls, and roads. Evidence of Roman greatness can be seen in lavish villas with ornate mosaic floors, temples uncovered beneath great English churches and Roman stones in medieval city walls. Roman roads sliced across the island in straight lines. Today any unusually straight small rural road is very likely laid directly on an ancient Roman road.

Roman Britain crumbled in the fifth century and there was little building in Dark Age England. Architecturally, the light was switched on with the Norman conquest in 1066. As William earned his title "the Conquerer," he built churches and castles in the European Romanesque style.

English Romanesque is called "Norman." The round arches and strong, simple and stocky style of the Norman (1050—1200) made churches that were fortress-like with thick walls, small windows and crenellations. Durham Cathedral and the Chapel of St. John in the Tower of London are typical Norman churches. The Tower of London with its square keep, small windows and spiral stone stairways is a typical Norman castle. You'll see plenty of Norman castles—all built to secure the conquest of these invaders from Normandy.

Gothic architecture (1200—1600) replaced the heavy Norman style with light and vertical buildings, pointed arches, tall soaring spires and bigger windows. English Gothic is divided into three stages. Early English (1200-1300) features tall simple spires, beautifully carved capitals, and elaborate chapter houses (e.g. Salisbury and Wells cathedrals). Decorated Gothic (1300-1370) gets fancier with more elaborate tracery, bigger windows, and ornately carved pinnacles, as you'll see at Westminster Abbey. Finally, the Perpendicular style (1370-1600) goes back to square towers and emphasizes straight uninterrupted verticle lines from ceiling to floor with vast windows and exuberant decoration including fan vaulted ceilings (King's College Chapel at Cambridge).

As you tour the great medieval churches of England, remember, nearly everything is symbolic. Local guides give regular tours, and books also help us modern pilgrims understand at least a little of what we see. For instance, on the tombs, if the figure has crossed legs, he was a crusader. If his feet rest on a dog he died at home, but if the legs rest on a lion he died in battle.

There aren't many Gothic castles. The rulers seem to have needed castles only to subdue the stubborn Welsh. Edward I built a ring of powerful castles in Wales (like Caernarfon and Conway) to deal with the Welsh.

Gothic houses were a simple mix of woven strips of thin wood, rubble and plaster called wattle and daub. The famous black and white Tudor, or half-timbered look, was simply heavy oak frames filled in with this wattle and daub.

The Tudor period (1485-1560) was a time of relative peace (the War of the Roses was finally over), prosperity, and renaissance. Henry VIII broke with the Catholic church and "dissolved" (destroyed) the monasteries leaving scores of England's greatest churches gutted shells. These hauntingly beautiful abbey ruins surrounded by lush lawns (Gladstonbury, Tintern, Whitby) are now pleasant city parks.

While few churches were built, this was a time of house and mansion construction. Warmth was becoming popular and affordable, and Tudor buildings featured small square windows and often many chimneys. In towns where land was scarce, many Tudor houses grew up and out, getting wider with each overhanging floor.

The Elizabethan and Jacobean periods (1560-1620) were followed by the English Renaissance style (1620-1720). English architects mixed Gothic and Classical styles, then Baroque and Classical styles. While the ornate Baroque never really grabbed England, the Classical style of the Italian architect, Palladio, did. Inigo Jones (1573-1652) and Christopher Wren (1632-1723) and those they inspired plastered England with enough columns, domes, and symmetry to please a Caesar. The Great Fire of London (1666) paved the way for an ambitious young Wren to put his mark on London forever with a grand rebuilding scheme including the great St. Paul's and over 50 other churches.

The Georgian period (1720-1840, the lousy German kings of England whom the celebrants of the Boston tea party couldn't stand) was rich and showed its richness by being very classical.

Grand pedimental doorways, fine cast iron work on balconies and railways, Chippendale furniture, and white-on-blue Wedgewood ceramics graced rich homes everywhere. John Nash, Jr. and Sr., led the way giving the trend-setting city of Bath its crescents and circles of royal Georgian rowhouses. England used to levy a window tax. Even the most elegant houses of this period had bricked-up false windows—one of the earliest tax dodges.

The Industrial Revolution shaped the Victorian period (1840-1890) with glass, steel and iron. England had a huge new erector set (so did France's Mr. Eiffel). This was also a romantic period reviving the "more Christian" Gothic style. London's Houses of Parliament are Neo-Gothic—just 100 years old but looking 1,000—except for the telltale modern precision and craftsmanship.

While Gothic was stone or concrete, neo-Gothic was often red brick. These were England's glory days and there was more building in this period than in all previous ages combined.

The architecture of our century obeys the formula "form follows function"—it works well but isn't particularly interesting. England treasures its heritage and takes great pains to build tastefully in historic districts and to preserve its many "listed" buildings. With a booming tourist trade, these quaint reminders of its—and our—past are becoming a valuable part of the British economy.

British TV

British television is so good —and so British—that it deserves a mention as a sightseeing treat (especially after a hard day of castle-climbing) over a pot of tea in the comfortable living room of your village bed and breakfast.

England has four channels. BBC 1 and BBC 2 are government-run, commercial-free and rather highbrow. ITV and Channel 4 are private, a little more Yankee, and have commercials —but those commercials are clever, sophisticated and a fun look at England. The public channels are funded by a $75 per year per TV tax—that's about 25 cents per day to escape commercials.

While California "accents" fill our airwaves 24 hours a day, homogenizing the way our country speaks, England protects and promotes its regional accents by its choice of announcers. British TV is limited to a few morning shows after breakfast, educational shows during a midday period, and a full slate of evening entertainment shows.

American shows are very popular—especially the "Dallasty" group, *Hill Street Blues, Cheers*, and *Cagney and Lacy*. Oldies like *Bewitched* and *I Dream of Jeannie* are also played.

The visiting viewer should be sure to tune in a few typical English shows. I'd recommend a dose of Archie Bunker-type fun with *In Sickness and in Health,* and the topnotch BBC evening news. For a tear-filled taste of British soap, see the popular *Coronation Street* or

Eastenders and, for an English Johnny Carson, see Terry Wogan's comedy show.

And, of course, if you like the crazy off-beat fun of Benny Hill and Monty Python—you've come to the right place.

Telephoning in Britain

Take advantage of the telephone. You can make long distance, or "trunk," calls direct and easy and there's no language barrier. I call ahead for rooms, to check opening hours, reserve theater tickets, and even to call home rather than mess with postcards.

The old pay phones take 10p coins. When you reach your number you'll hear the famous "rapid pips." Push in the coin and talk until you hear more pips which means it's time to sign off or pop in 10p more. Newer phones ingeniously take any coin from 2p to one pound and a display shows how your money's doing. Only completely unused coins will be returned, so put in biggies with caution.

Dialing 100 gets you the operator who can connect you with international assistance. 999 is emergency (free), 142 is London directory assistance, and 192 is assistance for other areas. The USA is 5 (east coast) to 8 (west coast) hours earlier than England time and direct calls cost about $1.50 per minute. Calls after 6:00pm are cheaper and there is no minimum time limit. I can get a ten-second message home for 20p.

Area codes for calling long distance are a headache. England has about as many area codes as we have prefixes. For local calls, just dial the 3 to 7 digit number. Area codes for "trunk" calls are listed by city on phone booth walls or through directory assistance. Area codes in Britain and Europe start with zero.

If dialing from another country, you replace that zero with the country code. For instance, England's country code is 42, London's code is 01. My London B&B's number is 727-7725. To call it from the USA I dial 011 (international code), 42 (British code), 1 (London), 727-7725. To call it from Brighton, I dial 01 (London) 727-7725. To call the USA direct from England, I dial 010 (international code), 1 (USA code), 206 (my Seattle area code) and the seven digit number. International calls are easiest on the new phones that take bigger coins.

Telephone Directory
Heathrow Airport departures—745-7067
US Embassy—(01)499-9000

CITY	AREA CODE	TOURIST INFO
London	01	730-3488
Salisbury	0722	334956
Bath	0225	62831
Cardiff	0222	27281
Stow-on-the-Wold	0451	30352
Wells	0749	72552
Stratford	0789	293127
Iron Bridge Gorge	095245	2753
Ruthin, N. Wales	08242	3992
Blackpool	0253	21623
Windermere	09662	4561
Keswick	0596	72645
Oban	0631	63122
Inverness	0463	234353
Edinburgh	031	557-2727
Durham	0385	43720
York	0904	21756
Cambridge	0223	358977
Dublin	01	747733

To dial USA: 010—1 (country code)—area code—seven digit number.
Costs about £1/minute, cheaper after 6:00pm and weekends.

Operator	100	London Dir. Assist.	142
Emergency	999	Outside London	192
International code	**010**		
USA	1	Germany	49
Canada	1	Italy	39
Belgium	32	Netherlands	31
France	33	Switzerland	41

Weather report, Lake District—(0532) 8092

The Anglo-Yankee Language Barrier
English —American
biscuit cookie
bonnet car hood
boot car trunk
cheers goodbye or thanks
chips French fries
crisps potato chips
dual carriageway 4-lane highway
fag cigarette
fortnight two weeks
jumper sweater
knock up wake up
loo bathroom
lorry truck
petrol gas
pissed drunk
queue up line up
stone 14 pounds weight
sweets candy
serviette napkin
napkin tampon or sanitary napkin
torch flashlight
pillar box postbox
1st floor 2nd floor
goose pimples goose bumps
candy floss cotton candy
off license can sell take-away liquor
take away to go
Building Society Mortgage Co., Savings & Loan Bank
Bookmakers shops for betting sports etc.
iron monger hardware store
chemist pharmacy
solicitor lawyer
estate agent real estate agent

BACK DOOR CATALOG

ALL ITEMS FIELD TESTED, HIGHLY RECOMMENDED, COMPLETELY
GUARANTEED AND DISCOUNTED BELOW RETAIL.

Back Door Combination Ruck Sack / Suitcase $60

At 9" × 21" × 13", this specially designed, sturdy functional bag is maximum carry-on-the-plane size. (Fits under the seat.) Constructed by Jesse Ltd. of rugged waterproof nylon Cordura material, with hide-away shoulder straps, waist belt (for use as a ruck sack) and top and side handles and a detachable shoulder strap (for toting as a suitcase). Perimeter zippers allow easy access to the roomy (2200 cu. in.) central compartment. Two small outside pockets are perfect for maps and other frequently used items. Two thousand Back Door Travelers took these bags around the world last year and returned satisfied. Comparable bags cost much more. If you're looking for maximum "carry-on size" and a suitcase that can be converted into a back pack, this is your best bet. Available in navy blue, black, gray, or burgundy.

Money belt..................................... $6.00

Required! Ultra-light, sturdy, under-the-pants, nylon pouch just big enough to carry the essentials comfortably. I'll never travel without one and I hope you won't either. Beige, nylon zipper, one size fits all, with instructions.

Sturdy Day Rucksack........................... $8.00

This lightweight, 8" × 16" × 4" blue nylon bag is ideal for day-tripping. Leave your suitcase in the hotel, on the bus, or at the station, and run around with this on your back. Folds into its own pocket.

Globetrotting $6.00

by Rick Steves (1985, 250 pp., retail $7.95)

A collection of 60 completely new Back Doors in Europe, Asia and the Americas. Over 250 fun to read pages laced with practical tips.

Eurail Passes Send Eurail form with check for the pass and a proposed itinerary and list of questions. Receive within two weeks train pass and free cassette tape-recorded evaluation of trip plans by registered mail. Because of this unique service, Rick Steves sells more train passes than anyone in the Pacific Northwest.

RICK STEVES BUDGET TRAVEL SEMINARS are taught to groups and colleges throughout the West Coast. Write for info.

All orders include: rubber universal sink stopper and a one year's subscription to our quarterly Back Door Travel Newsletter. Sorry, no credit cards. Send checks to:

"EUROPE THROUGH THE BACK DOOR"

111 4th Ave. N.   Edmonds, WA 98020   tel. (206) 771-8303

John Muir Publications

Europe 101: History, Art and Culture for the Traveler
376 pages, by Rick Steves
Finally, travelers have Europe 101! The first and only travelers guide to Europe's history and art. Full of boiled down, practical information to make your sightseeing more meaningful and enjoyable. Your "passport to culture" in a fun, easy to read manual.

Europe Through the Back Door
1986 Edition, Revised and Expanded, 382 pages, by Rick Steves
The lessons of 15 years of budget European travel packaged into 382 fun to read pages. All the basic skills of budget independent travel, plus 34 special "Back Doors" where you'll find the Europe most tourists miss. Sure to make you a seasoned traveler on your first trip.

Europe in 22 Days
Great Britain in 22 Days
Spain & Portugal in 22 Days
Rick Steves' *22 Day* series presents travel itineraries for the best three weeks each region has to offer. Each book supplies all the essential information you'll need, including city maps, train schedules, favorite bistros and small hotels, weather charts, a list of festivals, foreign phrases, and even a thumbnail sketch of the culture and history of the region.

Every day is treated as a separate unit and has a suggested schedule, sight-seeing, budget accommodations with addresses and telephone numbers and transportation notes.

And for travelers with less than three weeks to spend, the tour is designed so that you can start or stop at any point along the route.

Quantity	Title	Each	Total
	Europe Through the Back Door—*Steves*	$9.95	
	Europe 101: History, Art & Culture for Travelers—*Steves*	$9.95	
	Europe in 22 Days—*Steves*	$4.95	
	Complete Guide to Bed & Breakfasts, Inns & Guesthouses in the U.S. & Canada—*Lanier*	$11.95	
	The People's Guide to Mexico (Revised)—*Franz*	$10.95	
	The People's Guide to Camping in Mexico—*Franz*	$10.00	
	The On & Off the Road Cookbook— *Franz & Havens*	$8.50	

Send order to:

John Muir Publications
P.O. Box 613
Santa Fe, NM 87504

Subtotal	$
Shipping	$1.50
Total Enclosed	$